Why 27?

Why 27?

— how can we be sure that
we have the right books
in the New Testament?

Brian H. Edwards

EVANGELICAL PRESS

EVANGELICAL PRESS
Faverdale North, Darlington, DL3 0PH, England

e-mail: sales@evangelicalpress.org

Evangelical Press USA
P. O. Box 825, Webster, New York 14580, USA

e-mail: usa.sales@evangelicalpress.org

web: http://www.evangelicalpress.org

First published 2007

British Library Cataloguing in Publication Data available

ISBN-13   978-0-85234-650-1   ISBN 0-85234-650-6

Printed and bound in the United States of America.

Contents

Glossary of terms

Codex
Latin *caudex*, orig. 'a tree trunk' and later 'a ledger'. A manuscript bound in the form of a book rather than a scroll. The codex was being used by Christians before the year AD 70.

Coptic
The language used across Egypt in the Greek and Roman periods.

Cursive
Latin *curerre* 'to run'. A form of lower case writing in Greek. It was written more rapidly than uncial (capitals) and was used for everyday documents.

Majuscule (see uncial)
Literally 'large letters'.

Minuscule
Lower case (cursive) letters in Greek as opposed to majuscule. The letters are joined up or run together. Generally dated from the ninth century AD.

Nominen sacrum
Latin: 'holy name' (pl. *nomina sacra*). A term used for the practice of scribes abbreviating divine names for the persons of the Trinity. Generally the first and last letter of the word. Their use is early and mostly in codices.

Palaeography
Greek *palaios*, 'old' and *graphe*, 'writing'. The science of analysing handwriting in ancient documents.

Palimpsest
Greek *palin* 'again' and *psestos* 'rubbed' or 'scraped'. When writing material was in short supply or expensive, a parchment would be washed clean and reused. Modern technology often enables the scientist to read the original text. *Codex Ephraemi* (chapter 9) is a palimpsest.

Papyrology
Often linked with palaeography but covers the wider study of ancient manuscripts.

Papyrus
Paper made from the pith of the papyrus plant growing by the River Nile. Plural: papyri.

Parchment (see vellum)
Animal skin used for writing as opposed to papyrus (paper). Though often loosely used to refer to all writing material.

Pseudepigraphy
Spurious literature; from the Greek words *pseudes* (false) and *epigraphes* (writing).

Recto
Latin *rectus*, 'right'. The front side of a papyrus where the fibres run horizontally. See verso. A scroll was written on only one side whereas a codex would be written on both sides of the page.

Scroll
A length of rolled papyrus or parchment. Generally a scroll did not exceed more than 34 feet, though one reached 133 feet. The book of the prophet Isaiah would require a little more than the average and the Gospel of Luke just over 30 feet.

Uncial
Latin *uncia* 'inch'. An early form of capital letters used in many Greek texts chiefly from the third century on. However, forms of uncial are found in the first century. Some prefer the term 'majuscules' as opposed to 'minuscules' (see above). Generally uncial was used for more formal or dignified documents.

Vellum
Old French *velin*, a calf. Writing material made from the skin of young animals; it was therefore a smooth, high-quality parchment.

Verso
Latin *vertere*, 'to turn'. The reverse side of a papyrus where the fibres run vertically. See recto.

1. Entering the debate

The apostle Paul was a brilliant academic and he was never afraid to enter into a rational debate with his opponents. When accused of being out of his mind for defending his position by reference to the Hebrew Scriptures, Paul insisted that his arguments were both 'true and reasonable' (Acts 26:25). With equal assurance, the fiery apostle held 'discussions' daily in the lecture hall of Tyrannus at Ephesus (Acts 19:9), which meant that he both argued his case and lectured his hearers! Certainly Paul was confident of being able to 'demolish' the arguments of his opponents (2 Corinthians 10:5). His colleague Peter was equally insistent that Christians should always be prepared 'to give an answer' for their confidence (1 Peter 3:15) — just as a lawyer will defend his case in court — rather than rely on a dogmatic assertion of belief.

The purpose of this book is to enter the debate over the books that are found in the New Testament and to defend their right to be there.

To join some current discussions, one might be forgiven for assuming that the idea that there were other 'gospels' and associated writings in the early centuries of the church under the assumed name of the apostles is breaking news for the twenty-first century. On the contrary, 130 years ago B. Harris

Cowper published a book entitled *The Apocryphal Gospels and other Documents Relating to the History of Christ.* Naturally it cannot take account of some recent discoveries like the Nag Hammadi Library or the Gospel of Judas, but Cowper translated a number of the false gospels and letters and confessed: 'Before I undertook this work I never realised, so completely as I do now, the impassable character of the gulf which separates the genuine Gospels from these.'[1] Cowper concluded: 'They are of no historical or doctrinal authority, and were never officially recognised in the Church.'[2]

More than this, Cowper quoted the severe judgement of the nineteenth-century scholar, Dr Charles John Ellicott, writing some two decades earlier: 'From all alike — from orthodox fathers, from early historians, from popes, from councils, from Romanist divines and Protestant commentators — the same amount of contempt and reprobation had been expended on the Apocryphal Gospels, and yet they live and thrive, and are, perhaps, now as much and as curiously read as ever.'[3]

A century and a half later, they are not only read but are being turned into popular novels for the diet of an unaware and gullible public.

However, the subject is not always as straightforward as we would like it to be: if only Peter, John and Paul had left us a list of books to be accepted for exclusive use by the church. On the other hand, it is not quite as complex as the books and articles of some modern academics would want us to believe. In the middle of the nineteenth century, one of the most scholarly writers on this subject, Dr Brooke Foss Westcott, a Fellow of Trinity College Cambridge, and Bishop of Durham, claimed: 'From the close of the second century the history of the Canon is simple and its proof clear.'[4] That may be a little overstated, but there are few if any who have studied the relevant documents more carefully or written more thoughtfully on the subject than the learned bishop.

Entering the debate

The battle being fought today is age old. None of the documents that are the subject of so much public interest are new — nor is our knowledge of their existence new. Nothing should have taken us by surprise, though the media would not be expected to know this. The Nag Hammadi Library is a collection of books by Gnostic heretics, and the early church leaders were exposing their crude heresies and loose lifestyle well before the end of the first century. The Gospel of Judas is of interest only because now, at last, we have a copy of it — its existence has been known since Irenaeus wrote against it more than nineteen hundred years ago.

The attraction of these ancient documents lies partly in their hitherto secrecy — and everyone loves an open secret — but especially in their opposition to the New Testament gospel record and their strange and esoteric twist of the truth. From the apostles on, Christian leaders exposed these false writings.

A shift in the popular appetite

Modern writers who used the life of Christ as the basis for a novel at least took him seriously. *Ben Hur* by Lew Wallace (1888), Henryk Sienkiewicz in *Quo Vadis* (1896), *The Robe and The Big Fisherman* by Lloyd C. Douglas (1942) presented the public with a good read without damning the reliability of the Gospels.

All that has changed. From Nikos Kazantzakis in *The Last Temptation* (English translation 1961) to Gore Vidal's *Live from Golgotha* (1992) — a parody of the betrayal and crucifixion in which Jesus is rescued from the cross by a Japanese sun-goddess — to *Jesus Christ Superstar* (1971) and the blasphemy of Jerry Springer's *The Opera* (2005), the Gospels are trivialized or demonized. All this is to present a new and televised version of the life of Christ.

Irving Wallace in *The Word* (1972) was an early entrant into the field of disparaging the historical records of the four Gospels via a novel, and this was followed by the more serious attempt at research of Baigent, Leigh and Lincoln in *The Holy Blood and the Holy Grail* (1982), in which 'historical evidence' proved that Christ did not die on the cross but established a dynasty in the Merovingians, and that the legendary Holy Grail was the blood of this royal family. The theories of Baigent and co. were plundered by Dan Brown's *The Da Vinci Code* (2003) and its subsequent movie. The supposed 'scholarship' of Dan Brown's novel debunked the four Gospels as fourth-century inventions — as if the mass of true scholarly evidence did not exist.

However, there was nothing new in all this: *The Brook Kerith* by George Moore (1916) was an earlier version of the same poor imagination devoid of any historical evidence. Others, especially Gruber and Kersten in *The Original Jesus* (1995), have suggested that the teaching of Jesus is rooted in Buddhism. All this nonsense finds a ready market among a willingly gullible public and it is the only knowledge many daily commuters have of the canon of the New Testament.[5]

The smokers' corner

We are hardly surprised to find popular novels denouncing the Bible. Anything that criticizes the Bible pays well. Irving Wallace put into the mouth of George Wheeler the following pronouncement on the Gospels: 'These four Gospel writers had not lived with Jesus, observed him, seen him in the flesh. They had merely collected oral traditions, some writings from the early Christian community, and transcribed them on papyrus decades after the supposed death of Jesus. All this was frozen into the immutable canon that became our New Testament in the third or fourth century.'[6] And again: 'The modern biblical experts know that the present four gospels are not factual history... [they are] largely a series of myths strung together.'[7] Typically, of course, the 'experts' are hailed though no references are offered.

When Baigent, Leigh and Lincoln weighed in with *The Holy Blood and the Holy Grail* and the assurance that the Gnostic gospels 'enjoyed as great a claim to veracity as the books of the New Testament', and that 'The more one studies the Gospels, the more the contradictions between them become apparent',[8] we were reading a mixture of serious research and simple invention.

No sooner had we recovered from that, than Dan Brown in *The Da Vinci Code* claimed that 'More than eighty gospels were considered for the New Testament, and yet only relatively few were chosen for inclusion — Matthew, Mark, Luke and John among them'[9] and 'The Bible, as we know it today, was collated by the pagan Roman emperor Constantine the Great.'[10] Thus 'Almost everything our fathers taught us about Christ is *false*.'[11]

It has long been the leisure pursuit of novelists to rewrite the history of Jesus of Nazareth. But then, this is the age for revising history. Apart from Holocaust deniers, we can read a biography or watch a programme assuring us that neither Nero nor Pilate deserve the bad press they have received, and that Judas was in reality the hero of the crucifixion story. We wait only for some imaginative historian to assure us that King Henry VIII was not such a bad husband after all!

In the light of this, it is hardly surprising when a writer presents us with a popular novel that offers the veneer of history to persuade us that for seventeen hundred years the Christian church has been reading the wrong source book for the authoritative life of its founder.

However, it is a disturbing commentary on the level of academia at our red-brick universities when the Bible is petulantly dismissed by Prof. Richard Dawkins like this:

> To be fair, the Bible is not systematically evil but just plain weird, as you would expect of a chaotically cobbled-together anthology of disjointed documents, composed, revised, translated, distorted and 'improved' by hundreds of anonymous authors, editors and copyists, unknown to us and mostly unknown to each other, spanning nine centuries.[12]

Was that really the result of careful research by a professor at Oxford, or did Dawkins overhear it in the smokers' corner of a sixth-form common room? Not content, he continued:

> Ever since the nineteenth century, scholarly theologians have made an overwhelming case that the gospels are not reliable accounts of what happened in the history of the real world. All were written long after the death of Jesus, and also after the epistles of Paul.[13]

Certainly some *did* claim that in the nineteenth century, but this 'overwhelming case' is tired old theory now — as we shall see. However, our academic turns his attention to the Gospels:

> The four Gospels that made it into the official canon, were chosen, more or less arbitrarily, out of a large sample of at least a dozen... Nobody knows who the four evangelists were, but they almost certainly never met Jesus personally.[14]

At least Richard has reduced Dan's 'eighty' gospel contenders to 'at least a dozen'. But all this is mind-boggling ignorance from a professor at Oxford.

However, Oxford does not hold the pride of place in such academic foolishness. Back in the 1990s Barbara Thiering, for twenty-two years a lecturer at the University of Sydney Divinity School before her retirement, began publishing a cluster of books[15] in which she claims that Jesus was the leader of a radical faction of the Essene community, a major political movement to overthrow the pagan Roman Empire; he was not of virgin birth, did not die on the cross, was married to Mary Magdalene (whom he later divorced), fathered children who took an important role in the development of the new underground religion, and wrote the Gospel of John (with the help of Philip). He died some time after AD 64.

All this, and more, is claimed to be 'an historical account of the life of Jesus', but in reality it is the stuff of 'Holocaust denial'. If the subject had not been Jesus of Nazareth, it would surely have been hard to find a publisher. It must come in the same category as *Sacred Mushroom and the Cross*[16] in which Professor John Marco Allegro of Manchester University, England, claimed that hidden in the New Testament was a code for the Sacred Mushroom that was the real heart of the Christian faith.

The diet of 'scholarship'

At one time, few criticized the absolute trustworthiness of the New Testament and in particular the Gospel records. Their convictions gave rise to the well-worn idiom 'Gospel truth'. There were isolated sceptics of course. Back in the seventeenth century the Dutch theologian Baruch Spinoza investigated the Bible as an ordinary book: its date, context, authorship and setting. In the following century many ignored or even disparaged the Bible, like the third Earl of Shaftesbury's *Characteristics of Men, Manners, Opinions, Times etc.* that was very influential in its time. But it was hardly scholarly.

Why 27?

There was general agreement that the names that head the books in our English translations were either part of the earliest Greek texts that we possess, or they have a long and early tradition behind them. It was also accepted that the New Testament was completed somewhere between AD 50 and 100.[17]

However, by the nineteenth century all was to change. With the rise of biblical criticism, especially from Tübingen in Germany, the whole Bible was fair game for those who set out to discredit its reliability and therefore its message. Leading the pack was Professor Ferdinand Baur at Tübingen, who dismissed almost all the traditional views, and the following hounds tore into the New Testament. Most of the books were assumed to have been written around AD 150 and beyond, and the Gospel of John as late as AD 170. This cast serious doubt not only on the reliability of the New Testament text, but also on the actual canon of the New Testament. How do we know that the twenty-seven books are the right or only ones for our Bible? The short answer was that we could not.

Half a century on (around 1900), J. B. Lightfoot, a professor at Cambridge, dismissed the conclusions of Baur and set the dates much earlier. The German scholar Adolf von Harnack agreed. But still, most of the books were given a date well beyond AD 100 — making it impossible for any to have been written by or even with the knowledge of an apostle. However, few critics agreed with any of their colleagues as to the precise dates, authors or intended destinations of the New Testament books. The charge became a shambles.

Then, by the mid twentieth century, a significant change was discernable even among the most liberal critics. With the exception of 2 Peter (always an outcast and which was generally left alone in the cold around AD 125–150), most were considered to have been completed at least before AD 100. It can be seen, therefore, that those who still suggest a date for the New Testament books of between the second and third centuries are lagging somewhere around 150 years behind the progress of New Testament 'scholarship'.

Of course, there are always exceptions or else New Testament studies would come to a halt. In 1985 a group of around 100 scholars, under the leadership of Dr Robert Funk, met at the Pacific School of Religion in Berkeley, California. Known as the Jesus Seminar they set out to pool their scholarly research to discover how much of the Gospels could really be attributed to the precise days and words of Jesus. They circulated clever papers among themselves and met twice a year to vote on the sayings of Jesus. They voted by means of coloured beads. Red meant: 'That's Jesus alright'. Pink meant: 'It sounds like Jesus'. Grey meant: 'Well, maybe'; and black meant: 'No way'.

The fruit of their research came out in 1993 under the title of *The Five Gospels: The Search for the Authentic Words of Jesus*. Unsurprisingly from a group of liberal academics, only around 18% of the words of Jesus recorded in the Gospels could be classed as authentic or near authentic. Most of John's Gospel was black. Jesus did not consider himself to be the Son of God, nor did he anticipate his death as the purpose of his life. We could reduce the Lord's Prayer to 'Our Father' and the Beatitudes were lost altogether — and so on. *Time* magazine reported that just about all we know of the real Jesus, according to Dr Funk and his team, is that he had a disciple named Mary Magdalene, entered a synagogue at least once, and met some Pharisees. Fortunately there are not too many who take Dr Funk and his team seriously.

Redating the New Testament

In 1976 John A. T. Robinson, Dean at Trinity College, Cambridge, and recognized as a first-class New Testament scholar, published a book called *Redating the New Testament*.[18] That book sent shock waves through the academic world of New Testament criticism. Although, as a liberal and critical scholar, Robinson began his work as a 'theological joke', the evidence increasingly compelled him to take his own results more seriously. He finally concluded that the entire New Testament as we know it had been completed before AD 70. It is certainly a work of detailed scholarship in which every New Testament book is examined carefully.

Early in his research Robinson discovered that the greatest argument for an early date of the Gospels and epistles was the total absence of any reference to the 'single most datable and climactic event of the period — the fall of Jerusalem in AD 70'.[19] In this year, the besieging Roman army finally broke into the city, massacred its defenders and destroyed the temple. This would have been a conclusive vindication for the New Testament writers that God had finished with the 'types and shadows' of the Jewish ceremonial law. But there is not even a hint in any New Testament book that Jerusalem and the temple have been destroyed.

Robinson came to the conclusion that the only satisfactory reason for this silence is that the event had not yet taken place — a staggering conclusion for a liberal critic.

One reason most critical scholars placed the Gospels well beyond AD 70 was because these documents actually contained prophecies concerning the destruction of Jerusalem (e.g. Matthew 22:7; Mark 13:1-4; Luke 19:41-44; 21:20-24) — and the phenomena of prophecy could not be allowed. Even great minds in the prestigious universities of Europe overlooked the fact that you cannot prove a hypothesis by using that same supposition as your main piece of evidence.

There can, of course, be only one of three reasons for this significant silence:

- Either, the writers had not heard about the fall of Jerusalem — which would be at least odd since many of them lived in the city!
- Or, there was a massive and well-kept conspiracy that they would not refer to it — for reasons completely unknown to us and far beyond the imagination of any critic.
- Or, it had not taken place at the time the Gospels and epistles were written.

Elsewhere, Robinson wisely considered that it was a reasonable working assumption that the Acts of the Apostles could be trusted until proved otherwise. This assumption, he concluded, has been 'substantially vindicated'.[20] Consequently, the 'majority of English scholars' accept Luke's authorship of Acts.[21]

With painstaking care and methodical detail, Robinson examined every New Testament book to bring him to the inevitable conclusion that the entire canon was complete and circulating before the fall of Jerusalem in AD 70. Unfortunately, the man in the street — and apparently even Professor Dawkins — is unaware of these conclusions by a highly regarded scholar and liberal critic of the New Testament. They are equally unaware of the fact that, just to take one example, most scholars, from whatever their critical position, believe that Revelation, the Gospel of John and the three letters of John were all completed well before AD 100.[22]

Robinson was compelled to admit that 'There would seem to be a detectable swing back, if not to apostolic authorship [of the pastoral epistles] at any rate to taking seriously' the possibility of their being penned in the lifetime of Paul.[23] That, of course, leaves us with the amusing possibility that the letters claiming to come from Paul were written within his lifetime, without his knowledge, by person or persons unknown, whilst the great apostle himself has left us not a word to his credit!

'The tyranny of unexamined assumptions'

Equally as illuminating as the conclusions John Robinson came to regarding the completion of the New Testament books are his comments about so much modern scholarship. Remember, Robinson was a liberal critic who, to the day of his death in 1983, had no hesitation in denying John as the author of the Apocalypse, and had no idea who wrote 2 Peter. Many of the intellectuals he criticized are revered in the world of biblical scholarship. Yet Robinson commented: 'Datings that seem agreed in the textbooks can suddenly appear much less secure than the consensus would suggest.'[24] Elsewhere he claims: 'It is astonishing that so much has continued to be built upon so little.'[25] And again: 'It is sobering too to discover how little basis there is for many of the dates confidently assigned by modern experts to the New Testament documents.'[26]

He wrote of 'circular arguments' and 'presuppositions'[27] and deplored what he called 'disconcertingly tenuous deductions', 'sheer scholarly laziness' and 'the tyranny of unexamined assumptions'.[28] Perhaps the most damning comment is Robinson's perception of 'almost willful blindness' and 'the consistent evasion by modern commentators of a solution they have already prejudged to be impossible'.[29]

In defence of John the apostle as author of the Gospel that carries his name, Robinson comments: 'Most liberal scholars have allowed themselves to be insensitised, whether by the climate of critical opinion or for other reasons, to the very considerable strength [of the evidence] … for the apostolic authorship of the fourth gospel'[30]— and here he is sufficiently honest to admit his own earlier failure on this very point.

In a different but related context, Professor Carsten Thiede has commented that presuppositions are hard to abandon and that 'The instinct to undermine the Gospels has overtaken the pre-modern instinct to take their truth for granted… Some scholars and writers will go to almost any length to avoid the charge of credulity.'[31]

All of which makes Dawkins' confident affirmation that 'scholarly theologians have made an overwhelming case' against the reliability of the Gospels and Acts look, to be kind, a little fragile.

Academic myopia

That 'willful blindness' that leads many modern scholars to evade a solution 'they have already prejudged to be impossible' is easily illustrated. We have already noted that the presence of prophecy in the Gospels concerning the destruction of Jerusalem led critical scholars to claim that this must mean the Gospels were written after the event. Yet the silence in Hebrews of any reference to the end of sacrifices (which all agree was the case after AD 70) is claimed to have no significance in the dating of the epistle. In other words, the voice of prophecy is dismissed and the evidence of silence is irrelevant.[32]

Something similar is found in the debate about the authorship of 2 Peter. The main argument against it coming from the hand of the apostle is that the Greek is so different from 1 Peter. One scholar, J. B. Mayor, calculated that there were 100 words common to the two books and 600 different words.[33] That was in 1907. However, when in 1965 A. Q. Morton ran the two books through a computer, the conclusion was that the two epistles were 'linguistically indistinguishable' (in other words, very likely from the same author). Many liberal scholars simply responded that this only proved that the method of using computers was a waste of time![34]

Today, there is a new swing in favour of the evidence that the Gospels are not late writings but were penned early in the history of the Christian community and, notwithstanding the banal claims of recent popular novels and Oxford dons, the old idea that in the Gospels we cannot find the Jesus of history but only the whisper of the 'Christ of faith' — the faith of the third-century church — may at last be heading for its long-awaited grave.

Even the *National Geographic* magazine, in publicizing its recently deciphered (2005) Gospel of Judas, admitted that the four Gospels were written between AD 65 to 95[35] which, they claimed, was 'long after the death of the evangelists'. That was a most significant statement. At one time it was assumed by critical scholars that the Gospels were the figment of the wishful imagination of the third-century church; however, now that such a wild view is no longer tenable, 'between AD 65 to 95' is assumed to be 'long after the death of the evangelists' — without any supporting evidence that all the evangelists were deceased by then!

For any other portion of ancient literature than the New Testament, there is one particular piece of evidence that would be almost conclusive in favour of an early date for at least the Gospel of Luke and the Acts. Robinson saw it, but he was not the first. The exciting events that take place prior to Paul's arrival in Rome in Acts 28 lead us to expect some significant conclusion to the book. Here is the progress of action: arrest, lashing, inquisition, imprisonments, an appeal to the Emperor Nero, a shipwreck and miraculous rescue, and finally he arrives in Rome, is placed under house arrest and continues to share the gospel. The actual conclusion is a terrible anti-climax, and any reader with half a mind on what he is reading finds himself pleading: 'And then what?'

Why did Luke end here? There is no evidence of anything having been added or taken away from this ending. Only one reasonable explanation is available: when Luke penned Acts, the rest of the story had not been completed. Thus, if Acts was completed before AD 64 (the possible date of Paul's fate), the Gospel of Luke must be earlier.

If, as some have suggested, Acts was a sort of apologia for Paul in his defence and thus Luke did not want to show the emperor in a bad light, it amounts to the same thing. Besides, by AD 68 Nero was dead, and no one in the Senate mourned his demise — least of all his successors — so Luke need not have been squeamish in recording Paul's brutal end. Luke may well have died before the outcome of Paul's trial but clearly he had written his Gospel before Acts (Acts 1:1).[36] Anyone writing this story years later would most certainly have added an informative conclusion. In the event, Acts doesn't conclude — it just stops.

There is far too much evidence that the records in our New Testament are both accurate and early — very much earlier than some academics had previously allowed. But old theories die hard and many will wage a guerrilla war against any views that establish the trustworthiness of the New Testament canon.

The idea of a canon

It is a fact that whilst pagan religions vaguely share with Judaism and Christianity the idea of 'inspiration' from the gods, nothing in the ancient world religions compares with the clear Judaeo-Christian concept of a collection of authoritative books, compiled over many centuries, whose every word is considered to have a divine origin.

The word 'canon' comes from the Hebrew *kaneh* (a rod), and the Greek *kanon* (a reed). Among other things, the words referred equally to the measuring rod of the carpenter and the ruler of the scribe. It became a common word for anything that was the measure by which others were to be judged. In the ancient world the Greek authors were referred to as the 'canon' for the 'absolute standard for pure language'.[37] Paul used the word twice in the New Testament, at Galatians 6:16 and 2 Corinthians 10:13; similarly, the early church leaders used it to refer to the body of Christian doctrine accepted by the churches.

Perhaps Clement of Alexandria, early in the third century, was the first to employ the word to refer to the Scriptures (the Old Testament).[38] Origen also used it in the same century,[39] and Athanasius a little later. From here on it became more common in Christian use with reference to a collection of books that are fixed in their number, divine in their origin and universal in their authority.

Divine providence

If the early church leaders were concerned to know the identity of the writers of Scripture, they were equally concerned to recognize its divine origin. The New Testament is its own witness, not simply by its content, but by its claim. Our final appeal is not to man, not even to the early church leaders, but to God, who by his Holy Spirit has put his seal upon the New Testament. By their spiritual content and by the claim of their human writers, the twenty-seven books of our New Testament form part of the 'God-breathed' Scripture.

Anyone who has read even a little of the apocryphal and heretical writings produced in the first few centuries — and we will tiptoe into this dark realm in chapters 7 and 8 — will immediately see an enormous difference between these and the Gospels and the letters of the apostles.

The sixteenth-century French Reformer and theologian John Calvin expressed the significance of divine providence perfectly:

Nothing, therefore, can be more absurd than the fiction, that the power of judging Scripture is in the Church, and that on her nod its certainty depends... How shall we be persuaded that it came from God without recurring to a decree of the Church? It is just the same as if it were asked: How shall we learn to distinguish light from darkness, white from black, sweet from bitter? Scripture bears upon the face of it as clear evidence of its truth, as white and black do of their colour, sweet and bitter of their taste... Our conviction of the truth of Scripture must be derived from a higher source than human conjectures, judgements or reasons: namely, the secret testimony of the Spirit.[40]

In all our discussion about the formation of the canon of the New Testament, we should never lose sight of the relationship between the human and the divine. The pattern for this is the way in which the Scriptures themselves were written. The true meaning of the Greek word *theopneustos* in 2 Timothy 3:16 reminds us that all Scripture is 'God-breathed' — yet it came through men moved by the Holy Spirit (2 Peter 1:21). It is this harmony of the active mind of the human writer and the sovereign direction of the Holy Spirit that provides our confidence in God's inerrant and infallible word for the human race.

In the same way, we may discuss and recognize the various human factors in the formation of the New Testament canon, but we should never overlook the superintendence of God ensuring that finally only the books that he wanted would form part of the New Testament. Dr Carl Henry commented on this phenomenon of the divine intervention of God:

The first observation to be made in an objective survey is the remarkably extensive agreement with which the early church distinguished a particular and limited group of writings from all other literature ... and received them as uniquely inspired and of divine authority.[41]

John Wenham expressed the same truth: 'Grounds of canonicity are to be found in an interplay of subjective and objective factors overruled by Divine Providence.'[42]

It will be the contention of what follows to show that long before we have a directory of twenty-seven books, we have twenty-seven books being used as Scripture. Or, in the way Bruce Metzger phrased the question: 'Should the canon be described as a collection of authoritative books or as an authoritative collection of books?'[43] The first is correct. The books of the New Testament carried their own authority and because of this they were recognized by the churches. The authority resided in the books themselves and not in the lists that they later entered. Metzger describes the position like this:

> The books within the collection are regarded as possessing an intrinsic worth prior to their having been assembled, and their authority is grounded in their nature and source.[44]

Summary

- There is little about the false documents that have aroused so much public interest in recent years that is new for New Testament scholars.
- Books on biblical themes have shifted from a popular and positive read to a trendy and wholly negative read.
- Even some academics who should know better persist in trotting out worn mantras about the unreliability of New Testament documents.

Entering the debate

- The New Testament scholar, John A. T. Robinson, has presented a formidable case for the entire New Testament having been completed before AD 70.
- Robinson also vigorously objected to academic dishonesty, myopia, assumptions and scholarly laziness.
- The Judaeo-Christian concept of a collection of authoritative books, compiled over many centuries, whose every word is considered to have a divine origin, is unique among religious literature.
- Divine providence cannot be ignored when discussing the canon of the New Testament.

2. The Jews and their Bible

The Jews had a clearly defined body of Scriptures that collectively could be summarized as the Torah or Law. This was fixed early in the life of Israel and there was no doubt as to which books belonged and which did not. They did not order them in the same way as our Old Testament, but the same books were there. Strictly, the Law was the first five books, known as the Pentateuch which means 'five rolls'. The Prophets consisted of the Former Prophets (unusually for us these included Joshua, Judges, Samuel and Kings) and the Later Prophets (Isaiah, Jeremiah which included Lamentations, and the twelve smaller prophetic books). The Writings gathered up the rest. The total amounted generally to twenty-four books because many books, such as 1 and 2 Samuel, and Ezra-Nehemiah were counted as one.

In answer to the question: 'When was the canon of the Old Testament settled?' the simple fact is that we do not know. If we accept the reasonable position that each of the books was written at the time of its history — the first five at the time of Moses, the historical records close to the period they record, the psalms of David during his lifetime, and the prophets written at the time they were given — then the successive stages of acceptance into the canon of Scripture is not hard to fix. Certainly, the Jews generally held to this position. Clearly, when the Law was rediscovered in the time of Josiah it was accepted as having the stamp of God's authority upon it (2 Kings 23:3), but there is no reason to assume that this was the first time the Law had been accepted as Scripture.[1] We also know that it was customary for the words of the prophets to be written down (e.g. Jeremiah 36:2,4).

Most modern theories (and they are no more than theories) suggesting a late date for the final acceptance of the Old Testament canon rely on the equally fragile theories that the Bible books were written very much later than the periods they reflect. The suggestion that there was a threefold time sequence in the acceptance of the canon on the basis of the words of Jesus: 'Everything must be fulfilled that is written about me in the Law of Moses, the Prophets and the Psalms' (Luke 24:44) is without any foundation beyond speculation.

The Apocrypha and the Septuagint

The fourteen books of the Apocrypha (fifteen if the Prayer of Jeremiah is included separately from Baruch) were written some time between the close of the Old Testament and the beginning of the New. They were never considered as part of the Hebrew Scriptures; no one seriously suggested that they should be, and the Jews themselves clearly ruled them out by the confession that there was, throughout that period, no voice of the prophets in the land.[2] They looked forward to a day when 'a faithful prophet' should appear.[3] For the Jews, therefore, Scripture as a revelation from God through the prophets ended around 450 BC with the close of the book of Malachi.

Why 27?

Malachi was their last prophet, and he anticipated the second Elijah (Malachi 4:5), whom Jesus identified as John the Baptist (Matthew 11:13–14). The Apocrypha is chief among others that form various texts available during what is known as this 'intertestamental' period — between the testaments.

The Greek translation of the Hebrew Old Testament, the Septuagint, was begun around the middle of the third century BC. As Greek was still the common language across the Roman Empire, the Septuagint became the Old Testament text used by the apostles and the early church.

Although it is often claimed that the Septuagint contained the Apocrypha, there is no way of knowing this for sure since the earliest complete texts we have available are from the fourth and fifth centuries AD. Certainly these contain the Apocrypha, though in no particular consistency or order. But even if the Apocrypha was present, this did not mean that the Jews or Gentile proselytes to Judaism accepted it as part of the Hebrew canon any more than its presence in the Geneva Bible in the sixteenth century proves that the Puritans believed it was part of Scripture.

Significantly, whilst the apostles frequently used the Septuagint, they never once quoted or directly referred to the Apocrypha. They knew, as did all Jews, that it did not form part of the canon of the Hebrew Scriptures.

Some have found hints of the Apocrypha in the New Testament and claim this as evidence that the apostles accepted it as part of their canon; for example, Hebrews 1:3 may be a reflection of the Wisdom of Solomon 7:26 where wisdom is described as 'the brightness of the everlasting light, the unspotted mirror of the power of God, and the image of his goodness'. However, the reflections are often very tenuous, and even if they are deliberate allusions, as Wenham wittily points out: 'On such grounds, allusions in modern religious literature would canonize *Hymns Ancient and Modern*.'[4] Besides, it must be significant that although the apostles frequently quoted from the Old Testament and made their source clear, not once did they do the same with the Apocrypha.

Just as the Apocrypha was never part of the Scriptures recognized by the Jews, so it has never been accepted by the Protestant churches as authoritative in the same way that the canonical books are.[5] Not until the Council of Trent in 1546 did the Roman Catholic Church officially adopt some of the apocryphal books as 'canonical'.[6] However, to be accurate, the Roman position acknowledged the apocryphal books as 'deuterocanonical' (i.e. of slightly less status) whilst the Reformed churches accepted the Apocrypha as useful, but not to establish any doctrine. The Eastern Orthodox churches followed the Roman model, and added a few books not accepted by the Roman Church.

However, the earliest English translations of John Wycliffe (1380) did include the Apocrypha as a separate section, though with an introductory note that it is 'without the authority of the Bible', and the same was true of the Dutch (1526) and German-Swiss translations (1527–1529). William Tyndale did not live to complete the translation of the Old Testament, and therefore John Rogers, who compiled Matthew's Bible (1537) from Tyndale's work, simply added the translations of Miles Coverdale (1535) to complete the Old Testament and the Apocrypha; though Coverdale had been careful to note that the latter 'are not judged among the doctors to be of like reputation with the other scripture'.[7]

The Geneva Bible (1560) — so loved by the early Protestants and the Puritans — always included the Apocrypha until an edition appeared in 1599 without it. The Authorised Version (1611) originally contained it,[8] but by 1647 the *Westminster Confession of Faith* declared the Apocrypha to be no more than 'human writings'.

It is certainly true that the Apocrypha has had undoubted influence on the art and poetry of the west — familiar hymns such as 'Now thank we all, our God' and 'It came upon a midnight clear' were evidently influenced by passages in the Apocrypha. None of this lessens the evidence of the complete absence of any quotation from the Apocrypha in the Gospels or epistles, and the judgement of the Jews, the Reformers and the Puritans against its acceptance as Scripture. However useful some of the books of the Apocrypha may be as historical documents or even devotional aids, it is a serious mistake to add them to any volume of the Scriptures. The Jews certainly did not.

Josephus and Philo

Josephus (AD 37–100), the Jewish first-century historian who joined the revolt against the Roman occupation and then switched sides, clearly stated in his defence of Judaism that, unlike the Greeks, the Jews did not have many books:

> For we have not an innumerable multitude of books among us, disagreeing from and contradicting one another [as the Greeks have] but only twenty-two books, which contain the records of all the past times; which are justly believed to be divine.

As for the authority of these Scriptures, Josephus is clear:

> During so many ages as have already passed, no one has been so bold as either to add anything to them, to take anything from them, or to make any change in them; but it is become natural to all Jews immediately, and from their very birth, to esteem these books to contain Divine doctrines.

For this reason, 'No one has dared to add anything to them, or to alter anything in them.'[9]

Josephus was familiar with the Septuagint and made use of it. He listed the books, and continued that the reason why the same authority is not given to the history written after the time of Artaxerxes (Xerxes) is because 'there has not been an exact succession of prophets since that time'.[10] His twenty-two books are exactly the same as our thirty-nine in the Old Testament since, as mentioned above, many that we separate are counted as one book.

A little before Josephus, Philo (25 BC – AD 50) similarly comments that the Jews: 'have not altered even a single word of what had been written by him [Moses], but would rather endure to die a thousand times, than yield to any persuasion contrary to his laws and customs'.[11] Philo's writings reveal some two thousand quotations from the Pentateuch, and although he does not provide us with a list of canonical books, most of the Old Testament books are included in his work. He certainly never quoted from the Apocrypha.

The completion of the Hebrew canon at the time of Ezra is in line with the view expressed in the Talmud and other Jewish writings. The well-established tradition that around 400 BC Ezra collected the accepted books and had them accurately copied is confirmed by many scholars. John Wenham concludes: 'There is no reason to doubt that the Canon of the Old Testament is substantially Ezra's canon, just as the Pentateuch was substantially Moses' canon.'[12]

What happened at Jamnia?

Between AD 90 and 100, a group of Jewish scholars met at Jamnia in Israel to consider matters relating to the Hebrew Scriptures. We have no contemporary record of their deliberations and our knowledge is therefore left to the comments of later rabbis. It has been commonplace to assume that 'Here the books of the Jewish Scriptures were decided.'[13] But this idea that there was no clear canon of the Hebrew Scriptures until the 'Council of Jamnia' is not only in conflict with the testimony of Josephus and Philo, but has been seriously challenged more recently.

It is now generally accepted that Jamnia was not a council nor did it pronounce on the Jewish canon; rather it was an assembly (some prefer the word academy) that examined and discussed the canon. The purpose of Jamnia was not to decide which books would be included among the sacred writings for the Jews, but to examine those that were already accepted.[14]

In reality the team of rabbis that met at Jamnia seem to have spent much of their time discussing problems they had over Ezekiel (because they thought that he was not in line with the Law of Moses), Proverbs (because they could not reconcile some of the paradoxical proverbs), Ecclesiastes (because some considered it to be ethically unsound), the Song of Solomon (because it was being used as a secular song), and Esther (because there is no mention of God, and a festival unauthorized by Moses is established). The issue was not the right of these books to be *added* to the canon, but at the most, their right to *remain* there.

As a matter of fact there is no evidence that the issues that bothered the rabbis at Jamnia were a significant problem either to the Jews before them or to the generation of Christians after them — with the occasional exception, such as Martin Luther in sixteenth-century Germany and his problem with Esther which he wished had not been included!

One of the greatest Jewish scholars, Rabbi Akiba ben Joseph (AD 50–135), commented on the deliberations at Jamnia: 'If there has been any dispute, it referred only to Ecclesiastes.'

He himself considered that the Song of Solomon, which had been long accepted, was a 'holy of holies' among the Hebrew Scriptures.

Since the Hebrew Scriptures circulated as individual scrolls, it is not possible to say precisely when they were viewed as a complete and final body of sacred writings. However, what is certain is that well before the Qumran community, who copied what are known as the Dead Sea Scrolls from the middle of the second century BC, pious Jews recognized that the Scriptures were complete and that the voice of the prophets had fallen silent.

The Jewish Council of Jamnia in AD 100 may have argued over the contents of some of the books of the Old Testament, but they were not disputing the content of the canon. Nothing was written in or out at that time; the fact is, Jamnia simply confirmed what had been adopted throughout the history of Israel. The members did not define the canon, they simply re-examined it. In fact challenges to the canon among the Jews was unknown; in all discussions on record the issue was not to accept new books or exclude existing ones, but to confirm the status quo.

However, the Jewish scholars at Jamnia, like the later Christian leaders, had more material they could have chosen if they had wanted to. Apart from the Apocrypha, there were other writings around, such as the book of Enoch, the Psalms of Solomon and the Martyrdom of Isaiah — around seventeen books in all, according to one scholar.[15]

The Dead Sea Scrolls

The vast collection of scrolls, in various stages of terrible decay, that has become available since the discovery of the first texts in 1947 near Wadi Qumran close by the Dead Sea, may not help us greatly in our search for the canon of the Old Testament. No definitive list appears from the community and, even if it did, it would not necessarily tell us what mainstream orthodox Judaism believed.

However, all Old Testament books are represented among the Qumran collection with the exception of Esther, and it is generally agreed that the Law and the Prophets were regarded as authoritative Scripture. In fact, it is only the position of Ruth, Song of Songs, Ecclesiastes, Ezra-Nehemiah, Chronicles and Esther for which the evidence is insufficient one way or the other.

On the other hand, very little of the Apocrypha has been discovered, and it is never quoted in Qumran texts; the Qumran community wrote their commentaries only about biblical books.

In spite of suggestions by critical scholars to the contrary, there is absolutely no evidence, not even from the Dead Sea Scrolls, that there were any other books contending for a place within the Old Testament canon, or that any of our present books should not be there. On the contrary, all the evidence confirms an unbroken line of descent as the present books were added at their appropriate point in the history of Israel.

The Dead Sea Scrolls reflect something that is found in all Jewish writing at this time, and that is that whilst no list of canonical books is offered, whenever the canonical books are quoted or referred to, their authority is assumed. This is precisely what we find in the writing of the early church leaders: they do not provide us with a neat list of books that form the New Testament canon, but they quote and refer to them frequently and treat them — and only them — as authoritative.

The New Testament writers

For their part, the Christian community, both in the days of Jesus and in the centuries after, had no doubt that there was a body of books that made up the records of the old covenant. With almost twelve hundred direct quotations or clear allusions to Old Testament passages by Jesus and the apostles, it is evident what the early Christians thought of the Hebrew Scriptures. The New Testament writers rarely quote from other books and never with the same authority. The Apocrypha, as we have seen, is entirely absent in their writing.

They referred to the Old Testament books frequently, quoted from them often, and alluded to them continually; commonly with such introductory statements as 'the writing (or writings)'. Jesus set the pattern for his disciples when he claimed 'it stands written' (Matthew 4:4,6,10) and 'Scripture cannot be broken' (John 10:35). Beyond this, Paul had no doubt that the Jews were 'entrusted with the very words [the oracles] of God' (Romans 3:2). Carl Henry wisely concludes: 'The church inherited the Old Testament, and Jesus defended, encouraged and exemplified faithful submission to these writings as an inspired canon.'[16]

This position has been challenged in recent decades by the claim that the canon of the Old Testament was not fixed in the time of the apostles or the early church. However if, as some persist in suggesting, there was no clearly defined Old Testament before the meeting of the rabbis at Jamnia around AD 100, how can we account for the fact that the New Testament writers — whose Gospels and letters were all complete well before then — used the Old Testament books, and no other Hebrew texts, as Scripture? How could Jesus quote so regularly and authoritatively from a collection of books (and no others) that had not yet been recognized?[17]

The only time that an apostle quoted from a Jewish book other than the Old Testament was Jude's quotation from the Book of Enoch (only one third of which has survived and which is not part of the Apocrypha). Significantly Jude simply quoted from a piece of literature, does not tell us his source and certainly lays no claim to authority from it (Jude 14,15).[18] This is no different from Paul's brief references to the pagan writers Cleanthes (Acts 17:28), Menander (1 Corinthians 15:33) and Epimenides (Titus 1:12) — no divine authority is implied.

The early church and its Old Testament

The churches in the first three centuries were using the Septuagint for their Old Testament. The earliest copies of the Septuagint available today go back only to the fifth century AD and they include the apocryphal books. However, the original texts of the Septuagint clearly did not add all these books since it is doubtful whether they had been written so early. Besides, the apostles also used the Septuagint and they never once quoted from the Apocrypha and as we have seen, Josephus also used the Septuagint but limited the Hebrew canon to our thirty-nine books; all of which would imply that the earliest copies of the Septuagint contained only our thirty-nine books.[19]

Melito, Bishop of Sardis, is the first to provide us with a list of Old Testament books that many of the churches in the East were using, and it conforms to our canon. Origen, and after him Athanasius, both included the apocryphal Letter of Jeremiah as part of the prophet Jeremiah; although many scholars consider this was an oversight by Origen which was copied by Athanasius. Athanasius was clear that the Apocrypha, useful though some of it may be, formed no part of the divinely inspired canon.

Among the churches of the West, the picture is a little muddied by the fact that Tertullian, Bishop of Carthage, considered that some of the books of the Apocrypha, and even Enoch and the Sibylline Oracles,[20] might be inspired. The early church leaders were often far less precise in their terminology and therefore at times they may seem to attribute a divine origin to books that they did not consider to be part of the canon. Presumably they were unaware of the difficulty this would cause to later historians!

It was left to Jerome in the mid fourth century who, when he began to translate the Old Testament into Latin, recognized the wisdom of using the Hebrew Scriptures rather than the Greek Septuagint. In consequence, the books of the Apocrypha were not part of the canon. For his part, however, Augustine did include some of the apocryphal books, and the issue rumbled on throughout the Middle Ages until, as we have seen, eventually the Roman Catholic Council of Trent in 1546 endorsed the Apocrypha and the Church of England Thirty-nine Articles in 1562 rejected them.

To return to the early churches, whilst it is true that some of their leaders quoted from the Apocrypha, though rarely, compared to their use of the Old Testament books, there is no evidence that they recognized these books as equal to the Old Testament.[21] The conviction that there was a canon of old covenant books that could not be added to or subtracted from doubtless led them to expect the same divine order for the story of Jesus, the records of the early church and the letters of the apostles.

Summary

• The Hebrew Scriptures of the Jews were settled long before the time of Christ and the apostles, who also accepted their authority and frequently used them.

Why 27?

- The Apocrypha was never part of the Jewish Hebrew Scriptures, and the Jewish historians Josephus and Philo did not acknowledge the Apocrypha as Scripture.

- The Jewish Council at Jamnia discussed the contents of the books but not the content of the canon.

- The Greek translation of the Old Testament (the Septuagint) did not originally contain the Apocrypha but certainly later editions did.

- The Dead Sea Scrolls offer no list of accepted books, though all the Old Testament books are present (except Esther) and were considered authoritative. The books of the Apocrypha are largely absent and never quoted as Scripture.

- Jesus and the apostles quote constantly from the Old Testament, never from the Apocrypha, and the apostles only rarely quoted from pagan writers.

- Some of the early churches were confused over the limits of the Old Testament canon since they used the Greek translation that contained the Apocrypha.

- This acceptance of a complete canon of Old Testament books must have influenced the first-century church for a similar collection of Gospels and epistles.

3. The church and its Bible

According to Luke, even before the ink was dry on the scrolls of the apostolic Gospels, others were already drawing up their own account of 'the things that have been fulfilled among us' (Luke 1:1); but it was eyewitness accounts that mattered to Luke. His careful investigation (v. 3) was typical of the early church leaders who followed. They did not accept casually and thoughtlessly just anything that claimed to be apostolic. The evidence will show how careful the early church leaders were. This chapter is, in effect, a summary of all that follows. The conclusion drawn here is a result of the evidence which will be seen in the later chapters.

In answer to the question 'When did the church first have a Bible?' we can respond with certainty: it was never without one. From the very beginning the Hebrew Scriptures were accepted as the divinely inspired and authoritative word of God by the Christian communities; that part of the canon was accepted without question. The Hebrew Scriptures were 'the very words of God' (Romans 3:2). Thus 'The Christian church did not require to form for itself the idea of a "canon" ... it inherited this idea from the Jewish church.'[1]

The beginning of a New Testament canon

Long before the churches were eager to get hold of copies of letters from the apostles, those writers themselves were convinced that what they wrote was equal in authority to the prophets of the Old Testament. The prophets declared what was 'revealed to them', but equally the gospel was preached through the apostles 'by the Holy Spirit sent from heaven' (1 Peter 1:12). Similarly Paul was convinced that what he spoke was 'not in words taught us by human wisdom but in words taught by the Spirit' (1 Corinthians 2:13); which meant that his instructions were 'by the authority of the Lord Jesus' (1 Thessalonians 4:2).

There can be no doubt in the mind of anyone who reads the letters of the apostles, and the way they wrote about their own correspondence, that they knew themselves to be part of the continuing revelation of Scriptures given by men who 'spoke from God as they were carried along by the Holy Spirit' (2 Peter 1:21). Examples of this are Paul's clear linkage of Luke 10:7 with Deuteronomy 25:4 by introducing both with the phrase 'For the Scripture says' (1 Timothy 5:18) and Peter's attitude to the letters of Paul as equivalent to 'the other Scriptures' (2 Peter 3:16).

More than this, it is equally clear that the apostles expected their letters to be read and passed around the churches, even when the original was addressed to a particular congregation. Paul therefore instructed the church at Colossae to pass their letter to the Laodiceans and to obtain a copy of the letter he had sent there (Colossians 4:16). We may reasonably assume this became a common practice.

It is hardly surprising therefore to find one of the earliest Christian leaders following this precise pattern. Polycarp, who had been a disciple of the apostle John and was martyred in AD 155, wrote a brief letter to the church at Philippi and quoted from Ephesians 4:26 in the following way:

For I trust that you are well versed in the Sacred
Scriptures, and that nothing is hid from you ... It is
declared then in these Scriptures, 'Be ye angry, and sin
not,' and, 'Let not the sun go down upon your wrath.'[2]

Polycarp had no doubt that Paul's letter to the Ephesians was
'Sacred Scripture', and equally he assumed that the Christians
at Philippi not only believed the same but possessed a copy.

He also referred to the 'oracles' of the Lord, using precisely
the word that Paul had used to refer to the Hebrew Scriptures
in Romans 3:2. Clearly quoting from the first epistle of John,
Polycarp linked the 'testimony of the cross' with the 'oracles
of the Lord':

'For whosoever does not confess that Jesus Christ has
come in the flesh, is antichrist'; and whosoever does not
confess the testimony of the cross, is of the devil; and
whosoever perverts the oracles of the Lord to his own
lusts, and says that there is neither a resurrection nor a
judgment, he is the first-born of Satan.[3]

Possibly around the same time an epistle known as the
second epistle of Clement (which is generally considered
not to be from the hand of Clement) quoted from Isaiah and
followed it by: 'Again another scripture says, "I came not to
call the righteous, but sinners"', which is taken from Mark
2:17 or Luke 5:32.[4]

However, as we will see in the next chapter, whilst there is
evidence of all the New Testament books being used early in
the second century, there is no evidence yet of a definitive list
of books before the middle of that century. Equally significant
is the fact that the early Christian leaders clearly accepted the
New Testament Gospels and letters as divinely inspired and
therefore authoritative. The way they referred to the four
Gospels and the letters of the apostles, and quoted from them

in their own letters, reveals a uniqueness that is afforded to no other writings; and they often contrasted the authority of the Bible books with their own.

Polycarp referred to the writings of the apostles as the 'oracles' of the Lord, and Ignatius, who died as a martyr around AD 115, is typical of the way the church Fathers linked the 'Gospels and the Apostles' with the 'Law and the Prophets'. Writing to the Philadelphian church he commented:

> While I flee to the Gospel as to the flesh of Jesus Christ, and to the apostles as the presbytery of the Church. I do also love the prophets as those who announced Christ, and as being partakers of the same Spirit with the apostles ... The prophets and the apostles receive from God, through Jesus Christ, one and the same Holy Spirit, who is good, and sovereign, and true, and the Author of [saving] knowledge. For there is one God of the Old and New Testament.[5]

That reference to the 'New Testament' in the context of the Old is at least an indication of a growing collection of literature corresponding to the Hebrew Scriptures.

Similarly, to the Christians at Smyrna Ignatius wrote: 'but we should give heed to the Prophets, and especially to the Gospel, wherein the passion is shown unto us and the resurrection is accomplished'.[6] Whilst he does not name the 'Gospels' and the 'Apostles', Ignatius clearly possessed copies that would be recognized as such.

Ignatius wrote to the Magnesians: 'Do your diligence therefore that you be confirmed in the ordinances of the Lord and of the Apostles.'[7] There can surely be little doubt that here is a reference to known writings of the Gospels and the apostles.

When, a century later, Tertullian wrote of the Old and New Testaments, the Latin word he used was *instrumentum*, an instrument or tool. He referred also to 'The Law and the

Prophets, with the Gospels and the Apostles'.[8] Clement of Alexandria, a contemporary of Tertullian, made the same distinction.

All this is strong evidence that a developing canon of the New Testament was accepted long before a list of recognized books was drawn up either by the author of the Muratorian Canon around AD 150 (see chapter 5) or by Eusebius almost two centuries later.

In other words, the canon precedes the lists. By this is meant that before we have a directory of twenty-seven books, we have twenty-seven books being quoted and referred to as Scripture — that is a very important distinction. The canon as a formal list of books appears to have grown slowly over the first one hundred years of the Christian church, although the authority of most of the books that eventually composed the canon was accepted immediately by all but 'a respectable minority of the church'.[9]

The word 'canon' was not used to refer specifically to the books of the New Testament until sometime early in the fourth century when Athanasius referred to the Shepherd of Hermas as 'not belonging to the canon'. However, this implies that there was a clear idea of a canon before then. The thought was deep rooted in the church through its use of the Septuagint, and the apostolic writings were regularly read in the worship of the churches.

In the middle of the second century, Justin, in his *Apology to the Emperor Titus* (Antoninus Pius), outlined a typical Christian service at which:

On the day called Sunday, all who live in cities or in the country gather together to one place, and the memoirs of the apostles or the writings of the prophets are read, as long as time permits; then, when the reader has ceased, the president verbally instructs, and exhorts to the imitation of these good things.[10]

Although Justin does not mention it, other books were occasionally read at such meetings; these included the letters of Clement and the Shepherd of Hermas, but there is no evidence that they were placed on a par with the Gospels and the letters of the apostles, and they do not appear in the earliest lists of recognized books either. Carl Henry helpfully summarizes the situation like this: 'The first churches were therefore gifted not with a completed canon, but with a cumulative and culminating canon.'[11]

All this presupposes a recognition of what were the 'memoirs of the apostles'. That these books were collected together very early is beyond serious dispute. As we will see in chapter 9, the Chester Beatty Papyrus (P46) is the oldest collection of Paul's letters to date — ten of them — and it is dated around AD 200, though some have moved this date before the close of the first century.

Talk ... talk?

The tired old assumption is long past its sell-by date that for a long time the church had nothing but oral sayings of Jesus and that the stories of his ministry went the rounds growing in exaggeration until someone had the idea of writing them down. Unfortunately, it has been one of those untested assumptions that hopes to become more convincing the longer it is passed on. In truth, all the evidence runs the other way.

- There is good reason to believe, as we saw in chapter 1 from the work of J. A. T. Robinson, that most, if not all, the books of the New Testament were completed and circulating before AD 70.
- It defies logic to believe that an infant church, reared on the conviction that the Old Testament Scriptures are the very

words of God, should be satisfied with mere oral traditions for their own authority.

- If the churches were eager to obtain copies of the letters of some of the early leaders, as we know they were, how much more enthusiastic would they be to obtain copies of apostolic writing, especially with the precedent of Colossians 4:16 to spur them.

- The consistent quotations by the church leaders from New Testament books is clear evidence that they possessed written collections.

- The fact that they did not always give their source is no more surprising than when a preacher today quotes from the Bible without providing book or author. They were unaware that two millennia later scholars would be demanding a more exact code of reference.

Writing early in the fourth century, the church historian Eusebius described the way the apostles left the church a written record of their gospel, and there is no good reason to doubt the general truth of this claim:

> For Matthew, who had at first preached to the Hebrews, when he was about to go to other peoples, committed his Gospel to writing in his native tongue, and thus compensated those whom he was obliged to leave for the loss of his presence. And when Mark and Luke had already published their Gospels, they say that John, who had employed all his time in proclaiming the Gospel orally, finally proceeded to write for the following reason: The three Gospels already mentioned having come into the hands of all and into his own too, they say that he accepted them and bore witness to their truthfulness; but that there was lacking in them an account of the deeds done by Christ at the beginning of his ministry.[12]

However, we should never forget that even oral tradition in the first century was very different from today. Not only did Jesus promise the Holy Spirit to aid the apostles' memory (John 14:26; 16:13), in fact memories in the ancient world were far more accurate and receptive than today. Xenophon (the Greek historian and philosopher in the fourth century BC) tells of one Niceratus who, as a boy, learnt the *Iliad* and *Odyssey* of Homer by heart — all twenty-four thousand lines of them.[13] And that was not considered exceptional. Besides, during his three years of ministry Jesus repeated his teaching many times so that when his disciples went out preaching, they would accurately relay all that their Master had taught them.

The canon was complete when the last apostolic book was written, even though at the time the churches possessed no final list of these books. If we are to use the Muratorian Canon as our evidence, a canon of Scripture was evidently recognized by the mid second century; and it stayed that way for fifteen hundred years, until liberal critics in the eighteenth century — led by Johann Semler (1725–1791) whose presupposition was that the Bible was a book of fable — challenged this position. Even the doubts of Luther concerning the epistle of James and those of Zwingli concerning the Revelation of John found little acceptance with the churches of the Reformation in the sixteenth century.

If we ask how long it was before a complete list of twenty-seven books was recognized by most of the churches, the answer is: perhaps a little over one hundred years. But if we ask how soon it was before the canonical books were recognized by their recipients as authoritative, the answer is: immediately.

It must be emphasized that the earliest collections of books did not make them authoritative, they were collected because they were already authoritative among most of the churches. Significantly, in all the lists of accepted books, those Gnostic books discovered in the so-called Nag Hammadi Library in 1945 (see chapter 8) were never considered as candidates — simply because they were always known to be mischievous forgeries.

More clarity than confusion

One thing is certain, there is no evidence that the New Testament books came slowly to be recognized as authoritative and meanwhile jostled with an assortment of other literature before finally, after much wrangling and disagreement over a few centuries — and as much luck as judgement — they were accepted as canonical by church decree sometime in the fourth century. All the available evidence runs contrary to this.

The 'canonical' books were accepted immediately by the churches that received them, and whilst a few of the books were recognized more slowly in parts of the empire, the evidence from the letters of the early church leaders — and they have left many hundreds of pages between them — is that they knew perfectly well which books were 'apostolic' and which were not.[14] There is far more confusion among modern liberal critics than there ever was among the early church leaders. If they did not always use the words and phrases to describe them that we would like, such as 'inspired', 'inerrant', 'infallible', 'canon', 'final authority' and so on, this is because these did not form part of their vocabulary in this context. They do not often refer to the Old Testament Scriptures in this way either.

What is significant is that from the earliest times we find the church leaders constantly using what we know as 'canonical' books either by direct quotation, paraphrase or inference, to support their arguments or encouragements — and they rarely use other books in the same way. From the beginning, for example, it is clear that there were no other Gospels than the four used by the churches right across the empire. The exception, of course, was the Gnostic and other cults who invented their own stories (see chapters 7 and 8 for these); it is a matter of fact that none of these was ever a contender for a place in the canon.

But what of those books that were recognized more slowly in parts of the empire? In most cases the reasons for this are clear. The three most obvious in this category are the letter to the Hebrews, the second epistle of Peter and the Apocalypse of John. Hebrews was at first accepted but questions were raised at a later date among the western churches because the Montanists (an early group of extreme Pentecostals) used it widely in their teaching. 2 Peter was written in a form that many considered unlike Peter's style. And the Apocalypse similarly took longer to be accepted in the east because some were using it to support erroneous views of the millennium.

The modern idea that we cannot be sure of a completed canon and as a consequence we cannot have an authentic statement of Christian doctrine would certainly not have been tolerated by the leaders of the church in the first centuries. When eventually these leaders got round to stating which books had long been accepted as 'canonical', it was precisely to demonstrate where our authority is to be found, and to engage the heretics from that basis. Modern critics of the canon are successors, not of the stalwart leaders of the church in the first four centuries, but of the Gnostic and other deviants whom these leaders opposed.

Picking and choosing among the canonical books was not the task of the orthodox leaders, but of the heretics. It still is.

Which came first: the church or the Bible?

It is largely, though not exclusively, asserted by Roman Catholics that since the church came into existence before the

Bible, it must be the Bible that is dependent upon the church for its authority, and not the other way round. Certainly the church was in existence before all the books of the Christian Bible had been completed, but some significant points must be borne in mind:

- The same Lord who claimed that he would establish his church (Matthew 16:18) also promised that he would bring all things to the memory of the disciples for transmitting the truth (John 14:26; 16:13). His clear intention was for an authoritative and accurate Scripture for the church.
- At no point in the history of the church in the first four centuries did a council decide what books the church should and should not have; on the contrary, they simply acknowledged what the churches were already using widely. This is a significant difference. We shall see later that the New Testament books were accepted by the churches long before councils met to discuss the issue.
- There was a remarkable degree of agreement among the churches regarding the authoritative books, as the Muratorian Canon from the mid second century makes clear.
- We must never forget that the Christian churches unanimously, and yet without debate, adopted the whole of the Hebrew Scriptures as the first and indispensable half of their canon. It was precisely in this way that the Jewish canon itself had come into being — by use and not decree. It was only the Gnostic heretics like Marcion who dispensed with the Old Testament altogether. Even the liberal critic E. J. Goodspeed concludes: 'The church councils did not so much form the New Testament canon as recognize views about it that had taken shape in church usage.'[15]

How much more did the apostles write?

Clearly not all that the apostles wrote has been preserved. Paul wrote letters to the Laodiceans, the Corinthians and others that have not come down to us (Colossians 4:16; 1 Corinthians 5:9; and 1 Thessalonians 5:27), and the only two or three personal letters (Philemon; and 2 and possibly 3 John) are hardly likely to be the total of all private correspondence by the apostles. This also has its parallel in the Hebrew Scriptures. The Book of the Wars of the LORD (Numbers 21:14) has not come down to us and was never part of the canon of the Jews, nor was the Book of Jashar (Joshua 10:13) or the Book of the Acts of Solomon (1 Kings 11:41) which may have contained so much that is referred to in 1 Kings 4:32–33. There are many other missing books referred to in the Old Testament.

How and why these Hebrew books and apostolic letters were lost, from a human point of view we cannot usefully speculate on at this distance, but what we do know for certain is that the churches were eager to establish a body of books that would be normative for the life of the church across the known world. In each case it was the superintendence of the Spirit who chose which books would be of permanent value to the life of the church.

However, we must not assume too much. The first church historian, Eusebius, writing early in the fourth century, assured his readers that Paul wrote very few letters, and that of the seventy disciples sent out by Jesus, only Matthew and John have left us a record. Eusebius maintained that John wrote his Gospel only after he had seen the other three.[16] Whilst Eusebius is not necessarily reliable in all this, there is no firm evidence to doubt him.

When Carl Henry claimed in 1979: 'There is little probability that early manuscripts that the Christian community felt unobliged to copy and to circulate widely will now be recovered',[17] he would not have to retract that even in the light of the Nag Hammadi Library and the Gospel of Judas, for the simple reason that these false writings were never even considered for circulation by the orthodox Christian community; they were the preserve of recognized heretical sects. Henry is right to conclude that even if a text that came from the hand of Paul was discovered today, we would not add it as a supplement to the Bible, since the canon of Scripture is closed — and has been for almost two thousand years.[18]

Why did it take so long?

The autographs (the Gospels and letters penned by the original writers) of the New Testament were written between AD 48 and 70 (or AD 90 at the outside) and our first list of books does not appear until AD 150 in the Muratorian Canon. Why the gap in time if these books were considered to be Scripture immediately?

The impression can be given that the church across the empire was a cosy huddle with just a few bad guys at the fringe; that all the churches knew each other, had regular correspondence, acknowledged a limited number of leaders and by and large sang from the same hymn sheet because they all bought from the same bookstore in Rome. The reality was far different and there are many understandable reasons why it took some time for the twenty-seven books of the canon to gather in one place.

1. The churches were widely scattered across the empire and beyond.

By the time of the Edict of Milan in AD 313, in which Constantine legalized Christianity across the empire, there is evidence of churches already established in what we know today as Britain, France, Spain, North Africa (from Algiers and Tunisia across to Egypt and even down to Ethiopia), further east to Persia and back through Turkey and Greece to link with Italy. There is no reason to suppose that the church was not spilling even beyond these frontiers.

2. The New Testament books were written from different locations to different destinations.

We must never forget that the Gospels and letters were not penned by one writer in one location at one time and addressed to one church. From the beginning, the various books were scattered across the vast empire.

3. Communication would have been slow to some parts of the empire.

It would have taken some time for any one church to even learn about all the letters Paul had written, let alone gather copies of them. For example, the church at Antioch in Syria had first to hear that Paul had written to the church at Thessalonica — more than 800 miles and half a dozen provinces away — then they had to request a copy and wait for its arrival. And so on for all the twenty-seven books.

4. No scroll or codex could easily contain more than one or two books.

It would be impossible to fit more than one Gospel onto a scroll, and even when codices (books) were used, the entire New Testament would be extremely bulky and very expensive to produce.[19] It was therefore far more convenient for New Testament books to be copied singly or in small groups. The earliest complete New Testament in Greek (*Codex Sinaiticus,* see chapter 9) measures sixteen by fourteen inches.

5. The first-century Christians expected the imminent return of Christ.

Therefore they did not plan for the long-term future of the church. The idea of a collection of books would not have occurred to all the churches, especially those that anticipated the return sooner rather than later.[20]

6. The early church leaders did not write with future generations in mind.

By definition they were wholly ignorant of later debates over the content of the canon. That was not the issue. At first it could be assumed that when apostolic writings were quoted, this was a sufficient authority in itself. Why else were their letters and defence of the faith so full of quotes from the canonical books? All the converts accepted the Old Testament as the divinely given Scriptures for those under the first covenant, and the same authority was attributed to the Scriptures of the second covenant.

7. Only when the heretics attacked the truth was the importance of a canon appreciated.

It was not until the mid second century that the Gnostics and other deviants began making their own selection of which books they considered authentic (see chapter 7). Marcion, for example, accepted only Luke, Acts and ten of Paul's letters. This goaded the leaders to become alert to the need for stating which books had been recognized across the churches. Only when the authoritative books were attacked did they need to be defended. The leaders did not bother to scratch where the church didn't itch!

8. No one church or leader controlled all the others.

Although there were strong and respected leaders among the churches, Christianity had no supremo bishop who dictated to all the others. After the death of the last apostle, each church was wholly independent and its bishop fiercely guarded that independence. When the church at Rome first began to throw its weight around, it was decidedly put in its place by the others.[21]

9. For two hundred and fifty years the church was under constant threat of persecution.

Until the Edict of Milan in AD 313, persecution was at times severe. During the persecutions under Decius he set out to exterminate the church and demanded that all Christian books should be surrendered on pain of death. Paradoxically this both hindered and assisted the formation of a canon: the Christians were under siege, but needed to know which texts could be surrendered to the authorities as 'non-canonical'.

10. The early leaders assumed the authority of the Gospels and the apostles.

They did not see the necessity of repeatedly stating the obvious. They quoted from or alluded to the Gospels and apostles constantly in their writings, and that was apparently sufficient for the churches. They no more felt it necessary to keep on insisting on the exclusive authority and divine authorship of the Gospels and apostles than a modern-day writer does — inconvenient for us perhaps, but not significant for them.

The fact that, with rare exceptions, they only ever used the Gospels and apostles to support their arguments is sufficient evidence of their view that there was such a thing as a canon of authoritative New Testament books — even though for a century no one thought to make us a list.

In the light of all this, the marvel is not how long it took before the majority of the churches acknowledged a completed canon of the New Testament, but how soon after their writing each book was accepted as authoritative, how quickly a collection was recognized, and how widespread was the acceptance. It is remarkable that by AD 150 the Muratorian Canon, as we shall see, can provide a list very close to the one we are familiar with today.

It is true that it was not until the Council of Florence (1439–1443) that the Church of Rome, by then dominating Western Europe, finally settled the limits of the New Testament canon,[22] but that gives a very lopsided view of the subject. Centuries before this, the issue had been settled and all that remained were scattered sections of the church, the deviant cults and occasional individuals here and there who added or doubted the odd book or two.

However, to claim that this meant that the canon was still in a state of flux in the fifteenth century would be like saying that because the Mormons today insist on adding The Book of Mormon, The Pearl of Great Price and The Doctrines and Covenants to the twenty-seven books of the New Testament, then the canon is still not fixed in the twenty-first century. On the subject of the canon, the Mormons are hardly representative of the universal acceptance of the New Testament canon among Christian churches today.

The evidence at least confirms the claim that our acceptance of the canon of the New Testament does not depend upon the decision of the churches in a council of bishops. Scripture is its own witness and the early church leaders recognized this. Certainly there were no great conflicts among the early churches concerning the canon of Scripture; and when the heretics in the late second and early third centuries began to remove from the canon any books that did not suit their theology, the church leaders vigorously opposed them. Why, if the canon was still up for grabs?

In addition, all the evidence reveals that the early church leaders were far from gullible in their acceptance of Scripture. With so much material available, they were not quick to accept just anything claiming to come from the pen of an apostle. On the contrary, they were cautious and looked for the force of truth before they recognized the authority of a particular book. They were particularly careful to ensure the important apostolic authorship or influence upon any writing claiming to be Scripture.

Before we discover how often the early church leaders used the books that make up our New Testament, it will be helpful to gain an impression of what they themselves were writing for the churches, and this will be the subject of our next chapter.

Summary

- The early church accepted the idea of a fixed canon when it adopted the Hebrew Scriptures.
- The apostles knew that their writing was God-given and equal in authority with the Hebrew Scriptures.
- Long before our earliest existing list of books (c. AD 150), the early church leaders frequently referred to and quoted from the Gospels and epistles — and no others — as authoritative Scripture.
- Therefore, long before we have a directory of twenty-seven books, we have twenty-seven books being used as Scripture.

The authority lies in the books themselves rather than in the canon.

- By the middle of the second century the 'memoirs of the apostles' were being used regularly in Christian worship.
- The early Christians looked for apostolic authority to authenticate the canonical books.
- A handful of New Testament books, especially Hebrews, 2 Peter and Revelation, took longer to be accepted by some churches because heretical groups misused them.
- Given the conditions of the time, a list of recognized books was not slow in forming, but remarkably rapid.

4. A good read for the churches

The purpose of this chapter is not to outline the development of a canon of books among the earliest of the writers after the apostles — those known to history as the 'apostolic fathers' — but to introduce a sample of some of the best and most helpful writing of the time. For those readers interested only in the question of the canon, this chapter can be bypassed.

The rush of false gospels and pseudo epistles that circulated during the two hundred years following the death and resurrection of Christ threatened to overwhelm large sections of the church — and in some areas it succeeded. But it was not all gloom. Facing increasing persecution from the authorities and constant 'sheep stealing' from the heresies, many fluent and able leaders were busy writing to the churches in their care and defending the truth against the relentless attacks of the sects. In this chapter we will glance only at authors before the end of the second century; beyond then, there would be no possibility of new writings being considered for the collection of authoritative books.

These early letters, though mostly full of valuable instruction, might well have found their way ultimately into the canon of the New Testament — but none of them did.

Nor did their authors intend them to, and they were quick to distance their own authority from that of the apostles.

The second century was a busy time for writing, and this sample fairly represents the whole. It will also introduce some of the significant leaders of that time before we examine in the next chapter precisely how much of the New Testament canon they were familiar with.

The *Didache*

Discovered in 1875, the *Didache*, or the 'Teaching' of the twelve apostles, is possibly the earliest non-canonical Christian document on record. It is thought to have been written somewhere between AD 50 and 80 (though some scholars place it as late as the fourth century!), and its content is well in line with the New Testament teaching. Two clear quotations come from Matthew's Gospel, and other New Testament books are alluded to. It is not a book of theology but of practice, and as such was useful for the churches, although it adds nothing of any significance to the canonical books. Since it could not demonstrate an apostolic origin it was never accepted into the canon of the church; however, Athanasius thought it might be canonical, and Eusebius was equally certain that it was not.

The *Didache* deals with the Way of Life and the Way of Death (chapters 1–6); baptism, fasting and Communion (chapters 7–10); caring for travelling prophets and teachers (chapters 11–15); and finally (chapter 16) a brief warning about the coming Antichrist before the return of the Saviour.

Here are just two excerpts:

Thou shalt do no murder, thou shalt not commit adultery, thou shalt not corrupt boys, thou shalt not commit fornication, thou shalt not steal, thou shalt not deal in magic, thou shalt do no sorcery, thou shalt not murder a child by abortion nor kill them when born, thou shalt not covet thy neighbour's goods, thou shalt not perjure thyself, thou shalt not bear false witness, thou shalt not speak evil, thou shalt not cherish a grudge, thou shalt not be double-minded nor double-tongued.[1]

On the subject of baptism, clearly adult baptism is the only mode that is recognized:

But concerning baptism, thus shall ye baptize. Having first recited all these things, baptize in the name of the Father and of the Son and of the Holy Spirit in living [running] water. But if thou hast not living water, then baptize in other water; and if thou art not able in cold, then in warm. But if thou hast neither, then pour water on the head thrice in the name of the Father and of the Son and of the Holy Spirit. But before the baptism let him that baptizes and him that is baptized fast, and any others also who are able; and thou shalt order him that is baptized to fast a day or two before.[2]

The Epistle of Barnabas

For some, this epistle stood on what Metzger calls 'the fringe of the canon'[3] and it was tacked on the end of *Codex Sinaiticus* (one of our earliest complete Greek texts of the New Testament, see chapter 9) in the mid fourth century. However, by this time Eusebius had no hesitation in listing both Hermas and Barnabas among the books 'rejected' as having no part in the canon.

We have little idea of the date this was written, far less who wrote it, and none at all to whom it was intended. One scholar commented: 'It is generally regarded as impossible to accept the tradition which ascribes it to the Barnabas who was a companion of St. Paul, though it is convenient to continue to use the title.'[4] Clement of Alexandria was the first to ascribe it to the Barnabas of the New Testament — but Clement died around AD 216. Generally it is thought to have been composed late in the first or early in the second century. If the reference to the rebuilding of the temple in Barnabas 16:3–5 is taken to refer to the command of the Emperor Hadrian, as some do, then it must have been written after AD 130.

Apparently the old problem of the Judaisers that Paul had had to deal with had not gone away, and some were still insisting that Gentile converts should adopt many of the Jewish ceremonies. Barnabas, whoever he was, will have none of it, and in his attempt to dismiss the relevance of the Old Testament ceremonies, he indulges in some highly fanciful arguments. For example, he reasons that circumcision was never meant to be a sign of the covenant or else the Syrians, Arabians and even the Egyptians are all part of the covenant since they too practised circumcision.[5]

The writer employs even more fanciful allegorizing to escape the conclusion that Abraham circumcized his household of 318 males. Barnabas ingeniously interprets: 'In the eighteen "I" stands for ten, "H" for eight. Here you have JESUS (IHSOYS). And because the cross in the "T" was to have grace, He says also three hundred. So He reveals Jesus in the two letters, and in the remaining one the cross.'[6] Even the building of the temple was apparently a mistaken understanding of what God really meant.

However, it is not all like this, and there is some sound biblical reasoning as well. It closes with an exposition of the commandments and a warning against the deeds of 'The Black One'.

Whilst there is no reason to impugn the intentions of the author, since he makes no claim to apostolic association or divine inspiration, it is not hard to see why the book had only transient attraction among the churches. Its method is extravagant and at times trivial and foolish. It was relatively harmless, though not of great value to the churches and it proposed a novel and inaccurate interpretation of the Old Testament ceremonial law. Its chief appeal was that this kind of exaggerated spiritualizing was popular among many in the early centuries of the church.

The Shepherd of Hermas

Undoubtedly the most popular non-canonical book read among the early churches is known as the Shepherd of Hermas. The date of this book is still debated. There is some evidence for the author writing late in the first century and equal evidence for a date around the mid second century. The latter is more likely since the Muratorian Canon claims that it was written 'very recently, in our times, in the city of Rome' in the days when Pius (who died around AD 154) was Bishop of Rome. Evidence from the contents of the book would certainly agree with the later date, and it makes no claim to be apostolic, or even to have been written in association with an apostle.

As late as the fourth century Hermas was still used as an instruction manual for young converts and, together with the Epistle of Barnabas, it is attached at the end of the fourth-century *Codex Sinaiticus*. But by the close of the fourth century, Jerome claimed that although it was still used in Greece, it was virtually unknown among the western churches.[7]

Hermas is a slave in Rome who receives visions of the church in the guise of an old woman. The third vision is of a white tower, also representing the church, and it forms a parable of various types of people associated with the church, including leaders, the faithful, reprobates, the worldly and so

A good read for the churches

on. There is a strong warning against riches: 'When you were rich you were useless.'[8] Seven women supporting the tower are: Faith, Self-restraint, Simplicity, Guilelessness, Chastity, Intelligence and Love.

In the fifth vision we are introduced to the Shepherd who has been 'sent by a most venerable angel to dwell with you the remaining days of your life'. Hence the book is generally known as the Shepherd of Hermas. The Shepherd gives Hermas twelve commandments that exhort to Christian living and concludes: 'You have now these commandments. Walk in them, and exhort your hearers that their repentance may be pure during the remainder of their life.' Then follows ten 'Similitudes' (allegories) that come to Hermas from the Shepherd at various times.

The author certainly possessed a vivid imagination and he records his visions in great detail; it is a long read of over thirty-seven thousand words. Metzger describes the work as 'rambling' — it is certainly tedious — and the author as 'a simple man of limited outlook, but genuinely pious and conscientious'.[9] It may be hard for the modern reader to understand why it was so popular in the early church, although the visions and parables clearly appealed to many. There is nothing of particular error in it because it is fundamentally a book of good morality and stern self-discipline. However, there is little of the work of Christ or the gospel in it, and it has to be said that the Shepherd is stronger on morality than he is on theology. Perhaps the best way to describe Hermas is a mixture of the parables of the Old Testament prophets, the Apocalypse of John the Apostle, and the literature of Bunyan — without the authority of the first two or the clarity of all three!

The Muratorian Canon is clear that though Hermas may be read privately it should not be read in the churches since it is 'after the time' of the apostles.[10] For his part, Tertullian, later in the second century, was adamant that this book did not belong in the canon; it was: 'habitually judged by every council of Churches [even among the heretics] among apocryphal and false [writings]'.[11] Origen suggested, inaccurately, that the author may be the Hermas referred to in Romans 16:14 and even that it might be 'divinely inspired'[12] — but he was out on a limb on this.

Wise words from wise leaders

In addition to these anonymous documents, whose authorship and dates are still debated, there were many good and helpful letters written by the church leaders during the first two centuries in particular. They did not hide their authorship and made no claim to apostolic authority, and the churches did not consider them to have such either. There was never any question of them being confused with the canonical Scriptures.

Clement of Rome

The church at Corinth was in a mess — yet again! Paul had taken two or three letters to sort them out, but that was four decades ago. Paul had long gone, and although the apostle John might still be alive, it was left to Clement, the leader (bishop) at Rome, to send them a stiff correction for their bad behaviour. It would appear that the church had slipped back to the old bad habits that Paul had to deal with and, according to Clement, it was worse than before.

Clement is thought to have been the third Bishop of Rome, but we know virtually nothing about Linus and Anacletus who preceded him, except that Irenaeus mentions them and that Linus is the one referred to by Paul in 2 Timothy

A good read for the churches

4:21.[13] Because of the early date of the letter — somewhere around AD 96 — it is generally considered that he may be the Clement referred to in Philippians 4:3 as a 'fellow-worker' with Paul. Although Clement does not say as much, there are many references in his letter that imply a close association with Paul, and Irenaeus claims that he knew Paul so well and had listened to him so often that he 'might be said to have the preaching of the apostles still echoing [in his ears]'.[14]

It is not known for certain how Clement met his death, but one story is that he was tied to an anchor and thrown into the sea.

Clement began his lengthy letter by apologizing for not having written sooner — a common opener for correspondents in all ages — and set himself to attend to the issue on which they had sought his counsel, namely, 'the shameful and detestable sedition, utterly abhorrent to the elect of God, which a few rash and self-confident persons have kindled to such a pitch of frenzy'.[15] As any good pastor, Clement commended them for many good things at Corinth for which they are well known.

Sadly, however, their peace and humility, along with their reputation among the churches, has been shattered by division. Clement traced examples of division in the Old Testament and reminded the Corinthians of the sufferings and martyrdom of Peter and Paul, and others more recently. He then turned his readers to Christ: 'Let us look steadfastly to the blood of Christ, and see how precious that blood is to God, which, having been shed for our salvation, has set the grace of repentance before the whole world.'[16] And he promised them full forgiveness if they follow this path.

Throughout, the letter is thoroughly grounded in Old Testament Scripture with example following example and quotation following quotation; here and there the Gospels are used. He pleaded: 'Let us cleave, therefore, to those who cultivate peace with godliness, and not to those who

hypocritically profess to desire it.'[17] In detail Christ is put
forward as an example of humility, and this is followed by
the prophets who 'went about proclaiming the coming of
Christ'. Even the universe is held up as an example of peace
and accord:

> The sun and moon, with the companies of the stars,
> roll on in harmony according to His command, within
> their prescribed limits, and without any deviation …
> The seasons of spring, summer, autumn, and winter,
> peacefully give place to one another.[18]

Then the pastor addressed the various sections of the church:

> Let us reverence the Lord Jesus Christ, whose blood was
> given for us; let us esteem those who have the rule over
> us; let us honour the aged among us; let us train up the
> young men in the fear of God; let us direct our wives
> to that which is good. Let them exhibit the lovely habit
> of purity [in all their conduct]; let them show forth the
> sincere disposition of meekness… Let your children be
> partakers of true Christian training; let them learn of
> how great avail humility is…[19]

Clement continued by reminding them of the promise of
resurrection and the gospel of salvation by faith and not by
works: 'How blessed and wonderful, beloved, are the gifts
of God! Life in immortality, splendour in righteousness,
truth in perfect confidence, faith in assurance, self-control in
holiness.'[20]

Now, after a long haul, Clement came to the point. Just as in
the army 'All are not prefects, nor commanders of a thousand,
nor of a hundred, nor of fifty, nor the like, but each one in his
own rank performs the things commanded by the king and the

generals', and in the body 'all work harmoniously together, and are under one common rule for the preservation of the whole body', so it should be in the church.[21] Clement set out his order for the church: Christ was sent by the Father and in turn he sent out his apostles: 'Both these appointments, then, were made in an orderly way, according to the will of God.' It is this orderliness in the church that Clement appealed for, since that is everywhere the plan of God.

Clement is certain that those:

> ...who have blamelessly served the flock of Christ in a humble, peaceable, and disinterested spirit, and have for a long time possessed the good opinion of all, cannot be justly dismissed from the ministry. For our sin will not be small, if we eject from the episcopate those who have blamelessly and holily fulfilled its duties... We see that you have removed some men of excellent behaviour from the ministry, which they fulfilled blamelessly and with honour.[22]

The behaviour of such people is 'disgraceful' and 'unworthy' of their Christian profession.

Clement's final appeal must be in his own words:

> You therefore, who laid the foundation of this sedition, submit yourselves to the presbyters, and receive correction so as to repent, bending the knees of your hearts. Learn to be subject, laying aside the proud and arrogant self-confidence of your tongue. For it is better for you that you should occupy a humble but honourable place in the flock of Christ, than that, being highly exalted, you should be cast out from the hope of His people.[23]

It is little wonder that this powerful pastoral letter, so full of wisdom and Scripture, was still being read at Corinth decades after the church first received it.[24] It is therefore all the more significant that the letter of Clement to the church at Corinth was never a contender for inclusion in the canon.

Ignatius of Antioch

Ignatius was making his slow journey from Antioch to Rome under guard, knowing that at the end he would be thrown to the wild beasts for the sport of a roaring crowd. On his way, sometime in the year AD 115 and expecting inevitable martyrdom of the cruellest kind, Ignatius, known also as Theophorus, wrote six pastoral letters to churches, and one to his friend Polycarp. Those seven are the final testament of a condemned man. His letter to the Christians at Rome must have come as a painful prelude to what lay ahead:

> Let me be given to the wild beasts, for through them I can attain unto God. I am God's wheat, and I am ground by the teeth of wild beasts that I may be found pure bread [of Christ]. Rather entice the wild beasts, that they may become my sepulchre and may leave no part of my body behind, so that I may not, when I am fallen asleep, be burdensome to any one... Come fire and cross and grappling with wild beasts, wrenching of bones, hacking of limbs, crushing of my whole body, come cruel tortures of the devil to assail me. Only be it mine to attain unto Jesus Christ.[25]

This cluster of letters — that Polycarp later gathered and treasured and that the church at Philippi was so eager to obtain copies of — are full of pastoral care and good instruction, not least his warm and gentle letter to Polycarp. It is significant that this number of seven letters is greatly exceeded by the eleven that are listed as 'other spurious epistles in the name of Ignatius' — it was not only the canonical books that suffered from forgeries.

Ignatius was the bishop of the church at Smyrna, and in all his letters his theme is much the same: an encouragement to remain united under their bishop, and a warning of the many false teachers that were invading the churches and enticing people away. Writing to the Ephesians, Ignatius was anxious that he should not be judged as pretending to any superior authority — 'I do not issue orders to you, as if I were some great person'[26] — but he warns them against 'Some most worthless persons [who] are in the habit of carrying about the name of Jesus Christ in wicked guile, while yet they practise things unworthy of God, and hold opinions contrary to the doctrine of Christ.'[27]

In a similar letter to the Philadelphians he encouraged them to follow their leaders in the church and to be on their guard against false teachers; and with a clear stab at the growing influence of the Gnostics, he warned, 'If any one confesses Christ Jesus the Lord, but denies the God of the law and of the prophets, saying that the Father of Christ is not the Maker of heaven and earth, he has not continued in the truth any more than his father the devil, and is a disciple of Simon Magus, not of the Holy Spirit.'[28]

The Magnesians were warned against the Judaisers that were so troubling the church or churches addressed by Barnabas: 'Be not seduced by strange doctrines nor by antiquated fables, which are profitless.'[29] To his own dear people at Smyrna, Ignatius wrote from Troas and his gratitude for their prayers, love and provision of his needs, together with the fact that they were not ashamed of his bonds, is all a moving example of the relationship of a first-century pastor with his people.

Without exception these letters, which are not theological treatises but pastoral appeals, breathe the atmosphere of a Christian leader who is living close to God and whose spirit would encourage the churches to peace, harmony and truth. But again, the letters of Ignatius were never considered for inclusion in the canonical list.

Polycarp of Smyrna

It was Sunday 23 February AD 155 when the soldiers burst into the farmstead where Polycarp, the leader at Smyrna, had taken refuge. The old man of eighty-six years ordered a meal to be laid for the legionaries and invited them to eat and drink as much as they desired, while he spent just one hour in prayer before they took him away.

Arriving at the stadium in Rome, the proconsul, Statius Quadratus, urged Polycarp to have consideration to his age and to worship the emperor. This, according to *The Martyrdom of Polycarp*, was his reply: 'Fourscore and six years have I been his servant, and he has done me no wrong. How then can I blaspheme my King who saved me?'[30] When threatened with wild beasts, the old warrior replied, 'Call for them.' The proconsul warned of being burned with fire, and he was treated with the response: 'You threaten that fire which burns for a season and after a little while is quenched, for you are ignorant of the fire of the future judgment and eternal punishment, which is reserved for the ungodly.' As the soldiers were about to nail him to the stake, Polycarp requested: 'Leave me as I am; for he who has granted me to endure the fire will grant me also to remain at the pile unmoved, even without the security which you seek from the nails.'

So Polycarp died and his story was told and retold among the churches.

Polycarp had been a disciple of the apostle John, and apparently he wrote a number of letters, though only one has survived to date, his letter written to the church at Philippi. The church had evidently requested copies of the letters that Polycarp received from Ignatius who, on his own journey to martyrdom, was given hospitality at Smyrna by Polycarp. Polycarp was only too happy to respond to the request of the Philippians and sent copies by the hand of Crescens.

The letter contains no theology and adds nothing to the canonical books. However it is full of sound ethical instructions for the safety of the church.

Polycarp encouraged the Christians at Philippi to stand firm in the faith, avoid heresy and maintain a life of good works. He would also like to receive any news of the welfare of Ignatius — if he had not already died.

Polycarp was careful to distance his own leadership and authority from that of the apostle Paul; there was to be no danger of the Philippians equating Polycarp, or anyone else of his day, with apostolic authority:

> These things, brethren, I write to you concerning righteousness, not because I laid this charge upon myself, but because you invited me. For neither am I, nor is any other like unto me, able to follow the wisdom of the blessed and glorious Paul, who when he came among you taught face to face with the men of that day the word which concerns truth carefully and surely; who also, when he was absent, wrote a letter to you, into the which if you look diligently, you shall be able to be built up unto the faith given to you.[31]

Undoubtedly, the letter that Paul had written to the church at Philippi more than a century earlier was still a prized possession among them.

Papias of Hierapolis

Papias is a mysterious figure of whom we know very little except that he was leader in the church at Hierapolis in Phrygia, where Paul's fellow worker Epaphras had worked hard (Colossians 4:12–13), and that Irenaeus, who was writing in AD 180, claimed that he lived 'long ago' and that he was a friend of Polycarp; this means that he must have been alive at the turn of the first century. Only small fragments of the work of Papias have survived, which is frustrating since he wrote a lengthy *Expositions of the Sayings of the Lord*. He gathered most of his 'sayings' from word of mouth, but insisted that they had to be from the apostles.

Justin Martyr of Rome

In Justin, we have a very different kind of writing. These are not pastoral letters but a vigorous, even aggressive, defence of the Christian faith from a great mind steeped in the ability to argue a case well and forcefully.

Justin was a Gentile born in Samaria around the year AD 114. He was a philosopher by interest, education and practice, but it was the emptiness of philosophy — and he had tried most 'schools' — and observing the courage of Christians under torture and death that led him to Christ.[32] He was well travelled and spent time in Ephesus and Rome. It was in Rome that the philosophers plotted against him and he was martyred, probably when Marcus Aurelius was emperor.

Some of the most important, and certainly most voluminous writing of the second century comes from his pen. He wrote a lengthy work in defence of the Christian faith, addressed to the emperor and the senate, and a shorter protest against the treatment of Christians by a prefect; he also wrote an even more lengthy letter to Trypho the Jew, demonstrating that Jesus was the Messiah. These three are clearly his own work. However there are many other writings that are still disputed as to whether they belong to him or not, so it will be sufficient for us to limit ourselves to these works in summary.

The first appeal of Justin was addressed to the Emperor Antoninus Pius (AD 138–161), and through him to the whole Senate and the people. It was written between AD 153 and 155. Justin asked for justice and truth to prevail, citing the unfairness of Christians being punished simply because they bear that name, without any investigation. Let their lives be judged. They are charged with atheism for abandoning the national gods: 'And we confess that we are atheists, so far as gods of this sort are concerned, but not with respect to the most true God … we are not atheists, worshipping as we do the Maker of this universe.'[33] Justin quoted freely from the philosophers Plato, Socrates and others, and then, dangerously, showed the folly of worshipping idols which are 'soulless and dead'.

Justin defended the morality of Christians by quoting extensively from the words of Christ found in the Gospels, and included the Lord's encouragement to civil obedience. Then he turned his fire towards the immorality of paganism, including the cruel practice of leaving unwanted children to die on the mountains:

We have been taught that to expose newly-born children is the part of wicked men; and this we have been taught lest we should do any one an injury, and lest we should sin against God … there are some who prostitute even their own children and wives, and some are openly mutilated for the purpose of sodomy; and they refer these mysteries to the mother of the gods.[34]

All this is contrasted to the chastity of the Christians.

There is strong and vigorous criticism of the morality of paganism here, and perhaps Justin thought he had gone far enough, so he changed tack. It was now time to preach the gospel. He began with the Old Testament prophecies of Jesus — an issue he would deal with in vast detail in his debate with Trypho the Jew — and showed the birth, life, death, resurrection and ascension of the Messiah all in fulfilment of Old Testament prophecy. When he came to the cross, Justin carefully explained the purpose of Christ's death, but allowed himself a flight of fancy when he insisted that the symbol of the cross is all around us, from the sails of the ship, to the form of the plough and implements, to the human body erect and with outstretched arms. We can forgive this since he was writing for a first-century reader.

Justin's parting shot in his first *Apology* was to warn the emperor and the Senate: 'For we forewarn you, that you shall not escape the coming judgment of God, if you continue in your injustice.'

The second *Apology* is directed against the injustice of Prefect Urbinus; it is much shorter but no less potent:

If he assails us without having read the teachings of Christ, he is thoroughly depraved, and far worse than the illiterate, who often refrain from discussing or bearing false witness about matters they do not understand.[35]

Justin then went after the supposed thinkers, and demonstrated that both the Greek and Roman philosophers and poets were close to the truth when they mocked the gods and revealed the foolishness of pagan worship. Finally he appealed that his *Apology* should be published for all to read:

And we therefore pray you to publish this little book, appending what you think right, that our opinions may be known to others, and that these persons may have a fair chance of being freed from erroneous notions and ignorance of good ... And would that you also, in a manner becoming piety and philosophy, would for your own sakes judge justly.[36]

Whether or not the emperor read his defence is doubtful, but even if Titus Aelius Adrianus Antoninus Pius Augustus Caesar (as Justin styled him) took time out for a long read, it did Justin little good: around AD 165 he was condemned to death by Prefect Rusticus, and with six companions was tortured and beheaded.

Justin's theology is sound and his work is full of Christ. He showed himself to be a master at apologetics, even claiming that Plato gained his understanding of creation from the words of Moses,[37] and his work must have been a source of encouragement and ammunition for the Christians in their battle against Romans, heretics and Jews alike. But it was never a contender for inclusion in the canon of the New Testament.

Clement of Alexandria

Born in AD 153 Clement was a pagan philosopher, like Justin, but when he became a Christian he took on the mantle of one of the church's greatest teachers and apologists of the second century. A leader in the teaching school at Alexandria he turned that city into 'the brain of Christendom' until in 202 the persecutions under Septimus Severus forced him to flee. Somehow Clement survived the cruel years of the emperors Severus and Caracalla and he died, possibly in AD 216.

Clement is known especially for three works: the *Exhortation to the Heathen*, the *Instructor*, and the *Miscellanies*. His writing reveals his immense learning and at least one scholar has recorded almost 360 classical and other non-Christian authors quoted in his work.[38] Some of his arguments are found in the work of Justin Martyr, whom Clement had doubtless read.

The *Exhortation to the Heathen* was an evangelistic work to win pagans to Christ. The glory and purity of Christ is set out in contrast to the sordid licentiousness of paganism. It is a masterpiece of clarity and beauty in its composition, even though the orgies of the pagans are described in some detail. Clement did not spare the absurdity and cruelty of the pagan deities. Like Justin before him, he acknowledged that when both the high-minded philosophers and poets 'have given forth some utterances of truth, they bear indeed witness that the force of truth is not hidden, and at the same time expose their own weakness in not having arrived at the end'.[39]

The *Instructor* (or *Paedagogus*) is addressed to those who have turned from paganism and it is an encouragement to the development of Christian character and morality. It consists of three books and aims at the 'habits, actions and passions'. The first book exhibits Christ as our great Instructor who is 'God in the form of man, stainless, the minister of His Father's will, the Word who is God, who is in the Father, who is at the Father's right hand, and with the form of God is God. He is to us a spotless image.'[40]

The other two set out rules for the Christian life. Clement listed the ways the *Instructor* uses to correct his children, and it reads more like a thesaurus: admonition, upbraiding, complaint, invective, reproof, censure, denunciation, accusation and so forth! But always because he is the 'good Father'.

The instructions are detailed and practical, including eating and drinking: 'Some men, in truth, live that they may eat, as the irrational creatures, "whose life is their belly, and nothing else". But the *Instructor* enjoins us to eat that we may live.'[41] Even laughter is included: 'Pleasantry is allowable, not waggery.' Perfumes and jewellery are attended to, as is 'sleeping' and the kind of bed that should be used: 'stretching one's self on even couches, affording a kind of natural gymnasium for sleep, contributes to the digestion of the food'. Clothes, shoes, with whom to associate, and much more all find their place in Clement's careful instructions. It is all detailed and practical, and if it seems pernickety or even legalistic to us, we must read first his pleading with the pagan to leave a wasteful and licentious life and follow Christ, in order to understand where the young converts were coming from.

The *Miscellanies* (or *Stromata*), in eight books, sets out to defend the truth against the false teaching of the Gnostics. It presents a true Christian philosophy. The *Miscellanies* maintains that 'philosophy is the handmaid of theology'; in other words, it is merely a stepping stone towards the ultimate truth which is found only in Christ. But mere sophistry, a display of personal wisdom, is useless: 'To act well is far better than to speak well.'[42] Clement believed that there are fragments of truth in all systems, which may be separated from error; but that the truth can be found in unity and completeness only in Christ, since from him all the scattered gems originally came. In dealing with the Gnostics, Clement, with his massive store of knowledge from the philosophers and poets, demonstrated that the Gnostics are no more than Platonists in a new guise, and that true knowledge comes only from Christ.

Like Justin before him and Ignatius before that, Clement provided the church with strong arguments against both pagans and heretics but there was no question of any of his writings being added to the list of apostolic books.

Dionysius of Corinth

Dionysius is known to us only through the *Ecclesiastical History* of Eusebius. It is thought that he died around AD 170, but his birth date is unknown. This is the more surprising since he was an outstanding leader of the church in the second century and was Bishop of Corinth at the time of his death. He is remembered as a prolific writer of pastoral letters to various churches including Athens, Nicomedia, Lacedaemon, Crete and especially to Rome. Unfortunately only fragments of his letters have survived but Eusebius offers us a summary of seven letters from Dionysius.

From all that we can discover, it is clear that Dionysius was in line with orthodox teaching and his letters were widely accepted among the churches. It is Dionysius who tells us of the letter of Clement still being read.

Aristides of Athens

Little is known of Aristides and only in 1878 was a copy of his *Apology* discovered in an Armenian translation and, in 1888, a version in Syriac also. However, it was widely circulated in its day and was referred to as late as the ninth century. In his *Ecclesiastical History* Eusebius records that it was sent to the Emperor Hadrian and thus dated around AD 126, whilst others believe it was intended for Emperor Antoninus Pius which would date it after AD 138.

Aristides demolished the gods of the 'Barbarians' who set up 'gods of earth, water, fire, wind, sun and even men'. Then he turned his attention to the 'many fictitious gods' of the Greeks and then to the Egyptians 'because they are more base and stupid than every people that is on the earth'.[43] Finally there is a moving defence of the Christians and their life in fellowship with God and each other.

Athenagoras of Athens

Almost nothing is known about Athenagoras either, and his dates are equally uncertain. That he was a respected leader at Athens and wrote a number of works including *A Plea for the Christians* are about the only indisputable facts. Fortunately this work, written somewhere around AD 175, is available to us and it reveals an able and courageous scholar. In it he defended the Christians against the charges that they were atheists, ate human flesh at the Lord's Supper and committed incestuous sex.[44]

The Emperor Marcus Aurelius was the recipient of this stout defence from the scurrilous attacks, and such a treatise must have put heart into the new converts who found themselves criticized for the very things that were abhorrent to them.

The writer showed himself well acquainted with the Greek and Roman poets and philosophers, including Thales, Plato and Socrates. He quotes them to defend the unity of God as one, and yet showed that the Christian doctrine is superior even to theirs. In a strong defence of the Trinity, Athenagoras declared that polytheism is absurd; there follows a thorough demolition of the myths of the gods and of their incestuous relationships. It is, he suggests, 'nothing wonderful that they should get up tales about us such as they tell of their own gods'.[45]

By contrast the high morality of the Christians is open for all to see, and their approach to marriage is a model for others to follow. Their firm belief in the resurrection may be absurd to their accusers, but it is hardly a crime.

The final plea to the Emperor is worth quoting in full and it speaks for itself as a testimony to the quiet, peaceable and law-abiding submission of the early Christians.

> And now do you, who are entirely in everything, by nature and by education, upright, and moderate, and benevolent, and worthy of your rule, now that I have disposed of the several accusations, and proved that we are pious, and gentle, and temperate in spirit, bend your royal head in approval. For who are more deserving to obtain the things they ask, than those who, like us, pray for your government, that you may, as is most equitable, receive the kingdom, son from father, and that your empire may receive increase and addition, all men becoming subject to your sway? And this is also for our advantage, that we may lead a peaceable and quiet life, and may ourselves readily perform all that is commanded us.[46]

Irenaeus of Lyon

Until recent years, most of our information for the beliefs of the cultic groups and their literature came from the orthodox leaders who wrote against them. One of the most outstanding of these was Irenaeus who became Bishop of Lyons in France in the year AD 177.

Born in the Roman province of Asia (modern Turkey) around AD 130, Irenaeus lived for seventy years and he ranks alongside Tertullian as one of the most exact and clear-thinking theologians of the early church. Irenaeus tells how he himself often listened to the elderly Polycarp, who was martyred for his faith in AD 155, relating his conversations with John. Thus, Irenaeus was a 'grandson' of the apostles

A good read for the churches

and, according to the later historian Eusebius, he recalled the detail of Polycarp's careful reflections on the life and ministry of Jesus as he himself had gained it from John: 'Things that Polycarp had heard directly from eyewitnesses of the Word of life and reported in full harmony with Scripture.'[47]

When Irenaeus moved to Rome, he came into contact with two of the leading Gnostic heretics of the day: Marcion and Valentinus. We do not know why he later migrated to Lyons, but he had arrived at a busy cosmopolitan river port which had a population of some seventy thousand. Lyons was the provincial capital for Roman Gaul (France) and the centre for their transport system for the whole of the region. Christianity was well established here by the time Irenaeus arrived, but his passion for church planting meant that he learnt the local language. In his absence on one occasion, many Christians were martyred and he returned to a decimated and fearful church. The leader of the church, ninety-year-old Pothinus, was among those killed, and Irenaeus was elected to take his place in AD 177.

Within five years he had begun his monumental (five volumes) written attack against the heretics. It is known to us as *Against Heresies* (*Adversus Haereses*), though it was known in his time as *A Refutation and Subversion of Knowledge Falsely So Called*. His original Greek version has come down to us only in a Latin translation. He wrote other works, but it is *Against Heresies* that we will refer to here, since it is a clear refutation of the views of Gnostics like Marcion and Valentinus — with frequent quotations from their own work.

Until recently *Against Heresies* was a main source of information on the beliefs of the cults; however, with the discovery of the Nag Hammadi Library (see chapter 8), we now know how accurate Irenaeus was in relating their views. *Against Heresies* is much more than a refutation of error: it is also a clear statement of orthodox Christian truth.

Why 27?

This eloquent leader at Lyons could rightly claim to represent the church across the empire and beyond; he insisted that the same message was preached by all the churches and therefore it was incumbent on the heretics to show that the universal church was in error:

> The Church, having received this preaching and this faith, although scattered throughout the whole world, yet, as if occupying but one house, carefully preserves it... For the Churches which have been planted in Germany do not believe or hand down anything different, nor do those in Spain, nor those in Gaul, nor those in the East, nor those in Egypt, nor those in Libya, nor those which have been established in the central regions of the world... Nor will any one of the rulers in the Churches, however highly gifted he may be in point of eloquence, teach doctrines different from these.[48]

Irenaeus was aware of the subtleties of heretical teaching that made it so attractive to many:

> Error, indeed, is never set forth in its naked deformity, lest, being thus exposed, it should at once be detected. But it is craftily decked out in an attractive dress, so as, by its outward form, to make it appear to the inexperienced (ridiculous as the expression may seem) more true than the truth itself.[49]

Those who today follow the fashionable trend of defending the Gnostics and their work as supposedly reliable and reflective of the second-century church would do well to heed this warning. Indeed, such 'scholars' reveal more about themselves than about the true second-century church.

Precisely how and when Irenaeus died is uncertain, though the year 202 is probably close, and some traditions claim that he died a martyr's death. However, his legacy was excellent.

It is clear from this survey that the churches in the first one hundred years of its life after the last apostle had died did not lack educated and courageous leaders who could defend the truth against heretics, Jews, pagan philosophers and even the Roman authorities. Their work reveals men with a sound knowledge of the classics and philosophers, the Old Testament Scriptures and the writings of the apostles. Many of them breathe a warm pastoral heart, a clear academic mind and a strong understanding of the true gospel. Yet not one of them was a candidate for inclusion in the canon of the New Testament.

Our next point of interest must be to discover precisely how these early church leaders used the books of the New Testament.

Summary

- The churches were blessed with many able and wise pastoral leaders in the period immediately after the death of the apostles.
- They were careful to distance themselves from apostolic authority.
- They never wrote under assumed apostolic names but under their own name, though the *Didache*, for example, is anonymous.
- In their own time, there is no evidence that the churches ever accepted the writings of these early church leaders as equal in authority to that of the apostles.

- Their letters are very different from the literature of the Gnostics and their like. They are mostly plain, practical, pastoral and easy to follow. Even Hermas (with its wide use of allegory) and Barnabas (with its wild interpretation of the Old Testament) at least are not cloaked in mystery. No one could read both the Gnostics and the letters of the church Fathers without recognizing that they come from an entirely different family.

- The early defence of the faith against pagans by Justin, Clement of Alexandria, Athenagoras and Aristides reveals men of high intellect, well read in the classical literature of the day. Yet all, especially Clement, are evangelistic in their appeal.

- The church had equally able defenders against the Gnostic heretics especially with Irenaeus' *Against Heresies*.

5. What did the Fathers say? — the canon up to AD 180

In 1740 an Italian scholar, Ludovico Antonio Muratori, published a document he had discovered in a library in Milan. It was an eighth-century copy of an original written in Latin some time before the middle of the second century AD[1] and it contains our oldest known list of New Testament books reflecting the position held by the church in Rome at that time. Not all our canonical books are found in this list but none appears that ought not to be there — with one odd exception. The beginning and end of the copy is missing, and it begins with Luke as 'the third book of the Gospel'; clearly Matthew and Mark came first. The writer believed that 'all things are related by one imperial Spirit' in the Gospels.[2]

This Muratorian Canon not only lists the books of the New Testament, but adds comments on them as well, indicating their origin and acceptance. For example, Luke is endorsed as having been on the staff of Paul. It includes the four Gospels, Acts, thirteen letters of Paul, Jude, two (perhaps all three) letters of John and the Revelation of John. These are accepted by the 'universal church'. This leaves out: 1 and 2 Peter, James and Hebrews. However, 1 Peter was widely accepted by this time and may be an oversight by the compiler (or the later copyist).

The Muratorian Canon also includes the Wisdom of Solomon, though why this book that belongs in the Apocrypha should have been included here is anyone's guess, since there is no evidence that the churches were using it alongside the apostolic writings! A possible reference is made to the Apocalypse of Peter with a note that it is not widely accepted.[3] It contains also a list of heretical writers whose work is not to be used — these include Valentinus, Marcion and Basilides. There is a reference to Paul's epistles to the Laodiceans and to the Alexandrians (these two have not survived) as forgeries to further the teaching of Marcion, commenting: 'It is not suitable for gall to be mingled with honey.'[4] Perhaps the Muratorian Canon was in response to the condensed canon of the Gnostic leader Marcion who chose only the Gospel of Luke and ten letters from Paul for his 'canon'. The Shepherd of Hermas 'ought to be read' but not alongside the apostles.

This list in the Muratorian Canon, and its warning against dangerous books, is evidence of a growing directory of recognized books and the strong stand taken by the early church leaders against heresy — all within a century of the original autographs.

The witness of the early church leaders

We have already established that it was not a church council that decided on the books that would form the Bible; on the contrary, the church simply recognized the authorship and authority attached to the various books. This is seen very clearly when we compare what the early leaders said about themselves and their own writings with what they said about the New Testament books and those who wrote them.

Towards the close of the first century, Clement of Rome wrote a letter to the Christians at Corinth and he clearly had been influenced by the writing of Paul, but he makes no claim to apostolic authority; in fact, he writes as a representative of the church at Rome rather than in his own name: 'the Church of God which sojourns at Rome, to the Church of God sojourning at Corinth'.[5]

Ignatius was the leader in the church at Antioch around the year AD 112, not long after the death of the apostle John. He contrasted himself with Peter and Paul saying, 'I do not command you, as Peter and Paul did. They were apostles; I am a condemned man.'[6]

Polycarp of Smyrna, possibly the most influential church leader in Asia, tells us that he was a Christian by the year AD 70 and had actually sat under the teaching of the apostles. Before his martyrdom in AD 155 he referred to himself in this way: 'For neither am I, nor is any other like me, able to follow the wisdom of the blessed and glorious Paul.'[7]

Ignatius and Polycarp are typical of the attitude of almost all the early church Fathers. Dionysius of Corinth contrasted the Gospels and apostles with 'writings which are of less account'. These early leaders wrote scores of letters, many of which we still possess, but they never claimed the same inerrancy and authority for themselves that they gave to the New Testament books. Polycarp was sure that the apostles wrote with the same authority as the Old Testament prophets: 'Let us therefore so serve Him with fear and all reverence, as He himself gave commandment and the Apostles who preached the Gospel to us and the prophets who proclaimed beforehand the coming of our Lord.'[8]

How the New Testament books were accepted

The first list of New Testament books is found, as we have seen, in the Muratorian Canon, compiled somewhere during the mid second century. However, it would be inaccurate to assume that this was when the New Testament was formed. Although earlier writers do not give us an official catalogue of books, it is quite clear that they knew which books belonged to the body of apostolic authorship, although there is no evidence that any one of them possessed the full canon of twenty-seven books.

We should remember that these writers were not conscious of the debates that would arise centuries later on the origin of the canon; they were writing to resolve particular pastoral issues and what is significant is that in addition to extensive reference to the Old Testament scriptures, they also made constant use of the Gospels and apostolic writings and expected these to bolster their challenges, warnings and encouragements.[9]

The evidence to the close of the second century

The first four that follow are included for completeness, but, apart from Papias, they offer us little information on the development of the canon of the New Testament because they rarely quote from the New Testament. For most of those that follow, background information will be found in chapter 4.

The *Didache* (c. AD 50–80)

Possibly written late in the first century or early in the second, the *Didache* is a short manual of instruction to Christians, and although its existence was known about, until a copy was discovered in 1875 in a monastery in Constantinople we had no real knowledge of its contents. The significance for us is that there are two clear quotations from Matthew's Gospel (6:5ff and 7:6); there are also three other clear allusions to the same Gospel. Scholars are still divided over whether or not the *Didache* shows any knowledge of the letters of Paul.

The Epistle of Barnabas (*c.* AD 130)

Though highly regarded among the early churches, Clement of Alexandria and Origen are certainly incorrect in attributing this epistle to the co-worker with Paul since the destruction of Jerusalem had clearly taken place before it was written. As we saw in the previous chapter, Barnabas was of little value partly because of its extravagant interpretation of the Old Testament. The writer is equally unhelpful in quoting from the Wisdom of Solomon and 2 Baruch as if they are Scripture. However, one value of Barnabas is that in quoting widely from the Old Testament the writer also quotes from the Gospel of Matthew: for example 'many are called but few are chosen' and he introduces it by 'as it is written'.[10] Similarly he reveals a clear knowledge of 1 Peter and Romans in 'The Lord judges the world without respect of persons; each man shall receive according to his deeds. If he be good, his righteousness shall go before him in the way; if he be evil, the recompense of his evil-doing is before him.'[11] There are also echoes, but no more than echoes, of other New Testament books, especially the letters to Timothy.

The Shepherd of Hermas (*c.* AD 150)

As we saw in the previous chapter, both the authorship and date of this popular book are uncertain. Nowhere does Hermas quote directly from either the Old or New Testaments, though on many occasions the author reveals the influence of canonical books on his thinking, not least the epistle of James with which he was clearly very familiar. Hermas also appears to be acquainted with John's Gospel and Ephesians. He almost never quotes from other literature. However, the nature of his writing means that Hermas is of little value in assessing what was or was not accepted as canonical in his mind.

Papias of Hierapolis (AD 69–135)

Papias must have been alive during the lifetime of those acquainted with the apostles for he concerned himself with the quality, rather than the quantity, of oral traditions and in one preface he wrote:

> I shall not hesitate also to put down for you along with my interpretations whatever things I have at any time learned carefully from the elders and carefully remembered, guaranteeing their truth. For I did not, like the multitude, take pleasure in those that speak much, but in those that teach the truth; not in those that relate strange commandments, but in those that deliver the commandments given by the Lord to faith, and springing from the truth itself. If, then, any one came, who had been a follower of the elders, I questioned him in regard to the words of the elders — what Andrew or what Peter said, or what was said by Philip, or by Thomas, or by James, or by John, or by Matthew, or by any other of the disciples of the Lord ... For I did not think that what was to be got from the books would profit me as much as what came from the living and abiding voice.[12]

Sometimes his sources failed him. For example, Papias heard an odd account of the death of Judas: 'Judas walked about in this world a sad example of impiety; for his body having swollen to such an extent that he could not pass where a chariot could pass easily, he was crushed by the chariot, so that his bowels gushed out'[13] — apparently a case of first-century 'Chinese whispers'!

However, Papias does make reference to Matthew 'composing the sayings [of the Lord] in a Hebrew dialect', and he also commented on the Gospel of Mark (John Mark) compiled under the influence of the apostle Peter:

> Mark having become the interpreter of Peter, wrote down accurately whatsoever he remembered. It was not, however, in exact order that he related the sayings or deeds of Christ. For he neither heard the Lord nor accompanied Him. But afterwards, as I said, he accompanied Peter, who accommodated his instructions to the necessities [of his hearers], but with no intention of giving a regular narrative of the Lord's sayings. Wherefore Mark made no mistake in thus writing some things as he remembered them. For of one thing he took especial care, not to omit anything he had heard, and not to put anything fictitious into the statements.[14]

The one thing we may say with certainty is that Papias had access both to oral and written records of the life of Christ, even though he appears to have preferred the oral at this stage.

Elsewhere Papias shows that he was familiar with John's Gospel, 1 Peter, 1 John and Revelation. Whilst there are many New Testament books that Papias does not allude to, we must remember that he is both close to the apostolic age and yet distant from many of the other churches; it is very likely, therefore, that Papias had not yet received copies of all the letters of Paul.

Ignatius (AD 50–115)

The leader at Antioch — and possibly the successor to Peter himself according to some records — wrote seven letters on his journey to Rome where he was martyred around AD 115. His writing contains many clear references to New Testament books, and some scholars claim that he must have known almost the whole of our New Testament — though that claim is possibly a little exaggerated. There are few exact quotations because he is writing from memory and under the pressure of travelling as a prisoner, but Ignatius shows that he was acquainted with Matthew's Gospel and particularly quotes from John's Gospel.

Ignatius made wide use of the canonical books. For example, to the Ephesians he commented: 'And you are, as Paul wrote to you, "one body and one spirit, because you have also been called in one hope of the faith. Since also "there is one Lord, one faith, one baptism, one God and Father of all, who is over all, and through all, and in all."'[15] Clearly he possessed a copy of the very letter that Paul had written to the church at Ephesus that contained these words in Ephesians 4:4–6.

Ignatius was particularly impressed by Paul's self-effacing comments in 1 Corinthians 15:8–10, and on at least five occasions refers to himself as 'unworthy' or 'the very least'.[16]

Ignatius wrote to the Magnesians: 'Do your diligence therefore that you be confirmed in the ordinances of the Lord and of the Apostles.'[17] This appears to be a reference to known writings of the Gospels and the epistles.

Nowhere does Ignatius specifically refer to the texts he quotes from as 'Scripture', although it is certainly true that he demonstrates a wide knowledge of what we know as canonical books and used only those as his encouragement and authority with the churches.

Polycarp of Smyrna (AD 70–155)

In the letter from the leader of the church in Smyrna to the church at Philippi sometime after AD 110 some scholars have found fifty clear quotations from sixteen New Testament books, including Matthew, Luke, Acts, Romans, 1 Corinthians, Galatians, Ephesians, Philippians, 2 Thessalonians, 1 and 2 Timothy and Hebrews.[18] He quoted accurately from Matthew 7:1–2; 26:41; and Luke 6:36–38 and much more. Nothing can be read into the absence of some books since he may well have known them, but it served no purpose in his letter to quote from them. Westcott concludes: 'It is wholly unreasonable to doubt that he was acquainted with the chief parts of our Canon.'[19]

What is of particular importance is the fact that Polycarp frequently quoted in a way that implied the Philippians had access to the same written source. Thus he could introduce quotations by: 'Remember what the Lord said in his teaching…' and 'as the Lord has said'.[20] He also referred to 'the commandments of the Lord' and 'the oracles of the Lord',[21] which would have made little sense unless the churches had access to some written records containing the words of Christ. In each case he quoted accurately from the books as we know them. Among many quotations is this one that could have been taken from either Matthew 26:41 or Mark 14:38: 'as the Lord has said: "The spirit truly is willing, but the flesh is weak."'[22]

Polycarp was clearly very familiar with 1 Peter, which Bruce Metzger suggests 'he must have known practically by heart'.[23]

His short letter reveals a wide knowledge of the canonical books, for he quotes and alludes to them often, though without giving his source. It includes a reminder to the Philippians that Paul 'when he was absent, wrote a letter to you',[24] and a quotation from 1 Corinthians 6:2 is attributed to Paul.[25]

Polycarp referred only once to the 'Scriptures' in the context of a New Testament quotation: 'For I trust that you are well versed in the Sacred Scriptures, and that nothing is hid from you… It is declared then in these Scriptures, "Be ye angry, and sin not," and, "Let not the sun go down upon your wrath."'[26] But that single instance is highly significant. It is most natural to assume, in the light of his constant quotations from the New Testament, that it is not merely Ephesians 4:26 that is 'Scripture' but all the quotations he has given.

It is equally significant that although he warmly commends the letters of Ignatius: 'by them you may be greatly profited; for they treat of faith and patience, and all things that tend to edification in our Lord',[27] he never quotes from them to challenge or encourage the Christians as he does with the canonical books.

Polycarp became a Christian in AD 70 and was writing his letter early in the second century; he is therefore one of our earliest witnesses to the growing acceptance of our canonical books.

Clement of Rome (c. AD 95)

Clement was leader in the church at Rome before the close of the first century and his letter to the church at Corinth, written around AD 95, is of particular interest for us. He undoubtedly was familiar with Matthew's Gospel, and in his appeal to the church to leave aside its schism, Clement referred to Matthew 18:6–7, though without attributing his source but in such a way that assumes they have access to it:

Remember the words of our Lord Jesus Christ, how He said, 'Woe to that man. It were better for him that he had never been born, than that he should cast a stumbling-

block before one of my elect. Yes, it were better for
him that a millstone should be hung about him, and he
should be sunk in the depths of the sea, than that he
should cast a stumbling-block before one of my little
ones.'[28]

Clement did not feel obliged to quote exactly, and he
therefore adds phrases that do not belong in Matthew 18.
Perhaps Mark 14:19 and Matthew 24:24 are in his mind.

However, he was more specific when it came to Paul's letters.
Clement was well aware that Paul had written to Corinth on
the same issues and he assumed that the church possessed a
copy and that they would accept that it was written under the
inspiration of the Spirit:

Take up the epistle of the blessed Apostle Paul. What
did he write to you at the time when the Gospel first
began to be preached? Truly, under the inspiration of
the Spirit, he wrote to you concerning himself, and
Cephas, and Apollos...[29]

That phrase 'under the inspiration of the Spirit' (literally
'spiritually' or 'in the Spirit') is more than significant since it is
a clear indication that the churches not only possessed Paul's
letter to the Corinthians, but that they attributed to it divine
authorship. The way Clement writes here implies that already
the churches were gathering apostolic letters that they could
refer to as authoritative.

Similarly, Clement quoted from Psalm 118:18 and Hebrews
12:6 (though without giving either source) and described both
as the 'Holy Word'.[30]

In all, Clement reveals a knowledge (either by quotation
or allusion) of at least one of the Gospels as well as Hebrews,
Romans, Acts, Galatians, Ephesians, Philippians, 1 Timothy,

Titus, 1 Peter and James. Remember, Clement was writing before the turn of the first century. However, whilst he repeatedly introduces his Old Testament references as 'Scripture' he does not do the same with his quotations or paraphrases from what became canonical books. On the other hand, he uses them equally with the Old Testament to enforce his arguments, he considered Paul to have written under the guidance of the Spirit, and he referred to Hebrews as the 'Holy Word'.

The Second Epistle of Clement (c. AD 150)

This was not written by Clement and may well be the text of an early Christian sermon.[31] Probably dated around AD 150, the author is unknown.

The writer is clearly familiar with Matthew and Luke and at times combines quotations from each. Frequently he introduces his quotations by 'the Lord says'. On at least one occasion the writer added material to the Lord's reference to sending his disciples out like sheep among wolves. He was also familiar with 1 Corinthians and Ephesians. Occasionally, there is a hint of Gnostic ideas, and this is probably why the epistle was not widely circulated.

However, significantly the second letter of Clement quoted from Isaiah 56 and added, 'and another Scripture however says, "I did not come to call the righteous but sinners."' This quotation comes from Matthew 9:13.[32] This is an unusually explicit identification at this period and although this letter cannot be highly regarded, it does imply that positively equating the Gospels and apostolic writing with Scripture was already accepted by the mid second century, though we should not forget that both Paul and Peter had, long before, made the same identification (1 Timothy 5:18; 2 Peter 3:16).

Justin Martyr of Rome (AD 100–165)

Justin was one of the first and most capable of the Christian apologists who defended the faith to the Emperor and the Roman Senate. He was martyred in AD 165.

He does not quote by name from any New Testament writing, but he frequently used the four Gospels and employed the formulae of quotation 'it is recorded' and 'it is written', when quoting from the 'Memoirs of the apostles' or simply the 'Memoirs'. These memoirs, Justin tells his non-Christian readers, were called the 'Gospels'. In his first *Apology to Trypho the Jew* he quoted widely and accurately from the Gospel of Matthew in particular.

For the benefit of the emperor, Justin outlined the Christian Sunday services of worship during which:

> The memoirs of the apostles or the writings of the prophets are read, as long as time permits; then, when the reader has ceased, the president verbally instructs, and exhorts to the imitation of these good things.[33]

Interestingly, the Gospels are here placed in front of the prophets, and it is clearly assumed that the churches possessed, if not a complete, yet a significant collection of those 'memoirs'.

Justin was careful to distinguish those Gospels that were written by an apostle (Matthew and John) and those under the influence of an apostle (Mark and Luke). When he referred to Mark 3:16 (the name change of Peter), he referred to this Gospel as Peter's, which means that he followed the view of Papias that Peter was the apostle behind Mark's Gospel.[34] Similarly, when Justin quoted from Luke 22:42,44 (Luke was not an apostle) he noted: 'in the memoirs which I say were drawn up by His apostles and those who followed them, [it is recorded] that His sweat fell down like drops of blood while He was praying, and saying, "If it be possible, let this cup pass."'[35]

Occasionally Justin added a phrase or two to the Gospel text, but this does not necessarily mean that he had access to 'non-canonical' sources; perhaps he was simply elaborating as any preacher might. Only twice he offered two brief quotations from Jesus that are not found in the four Gospels.

In his long letter to the Jew Trypho, Justin made a clear reference to the book of Revelation and, whilst he did not quote from Paul, it would seem certain that he was familiar with the apostle's writing. He gave equal authority to the writings of the Gospels and apostles as he did to the Old Testament. It is common for him to introduce New Testament quotations with the phrase 'It is written', as for example Matthew 17:12: 'And it is written, "Then the disciples understood that He spoke to them about John the Baptist."'[36]

Justin's many references to the Gospels and apostles are often rough paraphrases rather than precise and accurate quotations; though there are many exceptions to this.[37] However, Bishop Westcott offers the interesting explanation that this actually indicates his familiarity with the text — he was so familiar with the sources that he did not bother to check the accuracy.[38] As a matter of fact, Justin was just as lax in quoting from the Old Testament and from secular writers.

Tatian of Rome and Syria (AD 110–180)

We know little about Tatian except that, according to the early Christian historian Eusebius, he was converted under Justin Martyr in Rome and later wrote a number of books in the middle of the second century, only one of which has survived. We do know that he compiled a harmony of the four Gospels, and this is known to us as Tatian's *Diatessaron*

— borrowed from the language of music referring to a series of harmonic tones and meaning literally 'through the four'. Only a fragment of this has survived, discovered in Syria as recently as 1933; it has the distinction of being the only New Testament document dated before the fourth century to be discovered outside Egypt — with the possible exception of 7Q5 (see chapter 10).

The *Diatessaron* is sufficient and important evidence to show that the four Gospels were in use and regarded as authoritative Scripture well before AD 150. More than this is the fact that some of the false gospels (for which see chapters 7 and 8) were already circulating by this time and yet Tatian ignored them all in preference for the four Gospels. This is perfectly in line with the practice of all the leaders during the second century whose records show that they used only the four.

The *Diatessaron* was very popular, particularly in Syria, and early in the fourth century at least two bishops had to order its replacement by the four Gospels.[39]

Unfortunately this clear acceptance of the four Gospels by Tatian was not followed by a full acceptance of the letters of Paul: he rejected some, but this was because they did not line up with his own peculiar eccentricity of theology which included rejecting eating meat, drinking wine and getting married. However, Tatian was clearly aware of many other epistles and used them positively.

Dionysius of Corinth (*c.* AD 165)

Sadly we have only fragments of the helpful letters that Dionysius wrote to several churches in the middle of the second century, but he offers a significant comment that the heretics ('apostles of the devil') had taken his letters and changed and twisted them ('taking away some things and adding others'); he concluded:

> It is, therefore, not to be wondered at if some have attempted to adulterate the Scriptures ('writings') of the Lord also, since they have formed designs even against writings which are of less accounts.[40]

Dionysius wrote firmly against the Gnostics, and Marcion in particular was probably guilty of interfering with his texts. Notice here that although Dionysius, in what remains of his writing, does not often refer to the Gospels and apostles, yet he is clear that what he writes is 'of less account' than those that carry the authority of the Lord himself. Obviously he expected his readers to concur with this high view of the Gospels and apostles.

Aristides (c. AD 126) and Athenagoras (c. AD 133–190) of Athens

Aristides wrote his *Apology* somewhere around AD 126 and addressed it to the Emperor Hadrian. He does not quote from the New Testament books, though his language at times is clearly influenced by the epistles, and in one significant phrase he directs the Emperor to a book of the Gospel that the King could read for himself if he wished: 'This is taught in the gospel, as it is called, which a short time was preached among them; and you also if you will read therein, may perceive the power which belongs to it.'[41] Towards the end he declares: 'Take, then, their [Christian] writings, and read therein, and lo! you will find that I have not put forth these things on my own authority.'[42]

It is tempting, though fruitless, to speculate that a copy of that Gospel may have accompanied this appeal!

Athenagoras wrote *A Plea for the Christians* to the Emperor Marcus Aurelius around AD 170. This brief but able defence of the faith was not too dissimilar from that of Aristides and he may well have had access to it. He uses both the Old Testament books and the Gospels and epistles sparingly. Certainly there are references to Matthew, Mark and John and at least Romans, Galatians and 1 Timothy, but this does not mean he was ignorant of more. To the mind of Athenagoras, in writing to a pagan emperor it was unnecessary to use Scripture as his authority, and he wields instead the pagan philosophers and poets to demolish what he sees as the absurdity of polytheism.

Summary up to AD 180

- With one exception, all our New Testament books are found in either direct quotations or allusions in the writings of these 'apostolic fathers' up to the year AD 180. That single exception is 2 Peter. [43]
- Apart from James, Jude, 2 and 3 John, 2 Peter, Hebrews and Revelation all other New Testament books had been almost universally accepted by AD 180. Only a few churches hesitated over these seven.
- The Muratorian Canon around AD 150 is our earliest evidence of an approved and orthodox body of books that was identified as the New Testament canon of Scripture. It contains all but four of our New Testament canon.
- There is clear evidence that already the canonical books were being gathered by the churches. For example, Clement reminded the Corinthians of the letter that Paul had written to them; similarly Polycarp reminded the Philippians, and Tatian selected only the four Gospels to compile his harmony. From Justin's description of Christian worship, it is clear that many churches were collecting apostolic writing.

- Unlike the Gnostic and other false literature, the church Fathers did not make up new sayings of Christ or the apostles, though at times they loosely paraphrased the Gospels or apostles. Nor did they quote from any other writings in the same way.

- The only time the leaders refer to the words of Christ or the apostles we can trace them to texts within the canon as we know it. The spurious Second Epistle of Clement and two small quotations in Justin are exceptions to this.

- When they used the Gospels and apostolic writings, the leaders clearly expected these to bolster their challenges, warnings and encouragements. Quotations were introduced naturally and without explanation; their use was considered authoritative and there is no discrepancy between them. There was no contest or debate over the books, they were accepted without discussion.[44]

6. The growth of the canon — from AD 180 to 325

The second half of the second century saw an increasing use of canonical books in the writing of the church leaders. Spurred by the urgent need to instruct the young Christians in the face of growing persecution and the onslaught of the heretics, it was inevitable that there would be a greater awareness of the authority that underpinned the Christian faith. Even by the middle of the second century, at least twenty-two of the New Testament books were acknowledged as apostolic and authoritative throughout the churches right across the Roman Empire, even though, apart from the Muratorian Canon, no formal canonical list had been compiled.

Irenaeus and Tertullian form a bridge between the two centuries, but in considering the evidence of these two giants and others, we must never forget that they were fallible men whose theology in other areas was sometimes less than exact. For example, Tertullian later became a Montanist and Origen, though thoroughly Trinitarian in his theology, was too much influenced by Plato.

However, before we come to this, there is a moving and valuable story that is worth relating.

Why 27?

The Scilitan Martyrs (AD 180)

On 17 July 180, seven men and five women were on trial before proconsul Saturninus in Carthage. They had only to honour the emperor by throwing incense on his altar and they would be free. This they refused to do and politely rebuffed all offers to think again. In defence Speratus, one of their spokesmen, claimed: 'The empire of this world I know not; but rather I serve that God, whom no man hath seen, nor with these eyes can see. I have committed no theft; but if I have bought anything I pay the tax; because I know my Lord, the King of kings and Emperor of all nations.' All twelve were condemned and summarily executed. The whole story has come to us in a text of just over five hundred and forty words.

At one point in the trial the following exchange took place:

Saturninus the proconsul: 'What are the things in your chest?'
Speratus: 'Our customary books, and the epistles of Paul, a devout man, which belong with them.'

Here in North Africa, a group of ordinary Christians are carrying with them a collection of books which included the epistles of Paul, though which ones (perhaps all?) we are not told. Metzger suggests that these Scilitan Christians were clearly, from the procedure of the court, common working folk, and were hardly likely to be reading Paul's letters in Greek. Therefore we are left with the conclusion that well before the close of the second century a collected Latin translation of Paul's epistles was circulating in North Africa. There can be little doubt that the four Gospels were circulating in the same area in Latin also.[1]

Irenaeus of Lyons (AD 130–202) — see also chapter 4

Irenaeus, who had been a student under Polycarp, wrote five large books *Against Heresies* about AD 180. The 'heretics' chiefly in his sights were the Gnostics, who dispensed with the Old Testament and were very selective over which books from the new order they would accept. This compelled Irenaeus to declare his hand and make clear which books were generally accepted as carrying apostolic authority equal to that of the prophets in the Old Testament. His use of accepted books is therefore all the more valuable.

In *Against Heresies,* Irenaeus quoted from over one thousand passages covering most of the New Testament. The book of Revelation was clearly one of his favourites. The exceptions are Philemon, 3 John and possibly also James, 2 Peter, Hebrews and Jude — though of course this does not mean he did not know of them or did not accept them. He had no doubt that the Gospels and apostles were 'Holy Scripture'.[2]

One thing is very clear from Irenaeus and that is that the four Gospels, and none other, were the only accepted testament to the life of Christ:

> It is not possible that the Gospels can be either more or fewer in number than they are, since there are four zones of the world ... and four principal winds... So firm is the ground upon which these Gospels rest, that the very heretics themselves bear witness to them, and, starting from these [documents], each one of them endeavours to establish his own peculiar doctrine.[3]

His reasoning may be suspect, but his conclusion is clear: by the mid second century only the heretics tried to add to the four Gospels. The four, and these alone, were circulating widely by this time.

Why 27?

Following Papias and Justin, Irenaeus believed Mark was the 'disciple and interpreter of Peter'.[4] Against the heretics and their spurious writings, Irenaeus insisted that the true faith came through the apostles who handed it down in writing:

> We have learned from none others the plan of our salvation, than from those through whom the Gospel has come down to us, which they did at one time proclaim in public, and, at a later period, by the will of God, handed down to us in the Scriptures, to be the ground and pillar of our faith.[5]

Irenaeus continued that they were 'invested with power from on high when the Holy Spirit came down' so that they might have 'perfect knowledge' — that phrase was a certain dig at the Gnostics and their boasted wisdom and secret knowledge.

Irenaeus had no doubt that God was the author of both the Old Testament and the four Gospels and the New Testament letters. They are all clearly labelled 'Scripture' in his writing. Only his addition of the Shepherd of Hermas intrudes. For him, a book was canonical if it was written by or under the authority of an apostle, and if the churches generally had accepted it. On this basis, Irenaeus possessed a canon of New Testament books almost identical, though not quite, to ours — and that in the year 180.

Irenaeus was impressed at the unbroken line of Christian leaders from the apostle Paul who had carefully passed on the truth: 'This is most abundant proof that there is one and the same vivifying faith, which has been preserved in the Church from the apostles until now, and handed down in truth.'[6] Although he never provided his readers with a list of accepted books in the New Testament canon, he must have had such a list in his mind since, with the single exception of Hermas, he only ever used the canonical books for his authority in rebuffing the heretics. With the addition of 1 Peter, the books used by Irenaeus are the same as those in the Muratorian Canon to which he may have had access.[7]

Tertullian of Carthage (AD 155–220)

Perhaps the greatest theologian of the century, and a formidable opponent of the Gnostic heretics, was born in Carthage. Tertullian was a highly educated African who became a lawyer and moved to Rome where he was converted around AD 195. He later returned to his home town. At the turn of the century he joined the Montanists, a group of early Pentecostalists, and died sometime after AD 220.

Tertullian undoubtedly speaks not only for the African church, but for the church at large, and he complements the work of Irenaeus and takes the evidence for the canon a stage further. He allowed no distinction between the law, the prophets and the apostles; together they formed the rule of faith:

> The apostolic churches, in which the very thrones of the apostles are still pre-eminent in their places, in which their own authentic writings are read ... the law and the prophets she unites in one volume with the writings of evangelists and apostles, from which she drinks in her faith.[8]

Further:

> We lay it down as our first position, that the evangelical Testament has apostles for its authors, to whom was assigned by the Lord Himself this office of publishing the gospel... Of the apostles, therefore, John and Matthew

first instil faith into us; whilst of apostolic men, Luke and Mark renew it afterwards.[9]

When he wrote of 'the records of the faith'[10] there can be little doubt that Tertullian had a recognized collection of books in mind, and he carefully distinguished between the apostles (Matthew and John) and 'apostolic men' (Mark and Luke).

Tertullian considered Barnabas to be the author of Hebrews;[11] however, that made no difference to its authority since Barnabas was a close companion of the apostle Paul. Significantly, Tertullian did not accept the Shepherd of Hermas and claimed that it had been widely rejected by the churches — he called it 'the apocryphal "Shepherd" of adulterers'.[12]

As a lawyer, we are not surprised at his preference for the written word — what he refers to as 'the majesty of our Scriptures'.[13] In one of his works Tertullian wrote: 'But let us rather be mindful of the sayings of the Lord, and of the letters of the apostles; for they have both told us beforehand that there shall be heresies, and have given us, in anticipation, warnings to avoid them.'[14]

No longer do we have scattered quotations or allusions to New Testament books; Tertullian is perhaps the first serious expositor, and typical of his handling of Scripture is when he turned his attention to Paul's letter to the Galatians. He set himself to analyse the very words that Paul used:

The epistle which we also allow to be the most decisive against Judaism, is that wherein the apostle instructs the Galatians... It is clear enough in what sense he writes, 'I marvel that you are so soon removed from Him who has called you to His grace to *another* gospel' — He means 'another' as to the conduct it prescribes, not in respect of its worship; 'another' as to the discipline it teaches, not in respect of its divinity.[15]

In his defence of the true faith — what he referred to as 'the rule of faith' (*regula fidei*) — Tertullian used all the New Testament books except James, 2 and 3 John and 2 Peter; of Paul's letters, only Philemon is missing. However, this is no comment either way on his acceptance of those he omitted. He quoted from Revelation frequently, and ascribed it to John. There can be no doubt that Tertullian possessed a collection of books that he recognized as the regulators of faith, and it was likely to be almost, if not wholly, identical to our canon of the New Testament.

It is also evident from Tertullian that the Gospels and apostolic letters had already been translated from the Greek into Latin by his day. Tertullian was aware that Irenaeus had made such translations and this, by the turn of the second century.

Tertullian wrote at length about the apostles' authority and one brief quotation must be sufficient: 'In the Lord's apostles we possess our authority, for even they did not of themselves choose to introduce anything, but faithfully delivered to the nations the doctrine which they have received from Christ.'[16] He used the phrase 'New Testament' to refer to the second part of the Christian Bible.

Cyprian of Carthage (AD 210–258)

Born in AD 210, Cyprian was converted around AD 246, sold all his property for the poor and vowed chastity and poverty — within twelve years he had been martyred. He became an avid student of Scripture and especially of Tertullian. His brilliant mind meant that he was appointed Bishop of Carthage, the leading church in North Africa. Cyprian was a prolific writer, and much of his work has survived. One scholar has computed that he quoted in his letters from almost ten per cent of the New Testament![17] He does not quote from Philemon, Hebrews, James, 2 Peter, 2 and 3 John and Jude. This closely parallels with Tertullian and he must have known Hebrews because Tertullian used it frequently and there is at least one clear allusion to it.[18] All his quotations are prefaced with 'it is written' or 'Scriptures' or something similar. Once again, he refers to only four Gospels.

Hippolytus of Rome (AD 170–235)

We know little about the early life of Hippolytus except that he was born around AD 170 and studied under Irenaeus. On moving to Rome, he soon established his reputation as a preacher and writer. He was martyred for his faith in AD 235.

Writing between AD 200 and his death, he has more than forty works to his name, and they include commentaries on Scripture and Christian doctrine. He wrote ten books on *A Refutation of all Heresies.* Sadly little has survived but it appears that his 'canon' was almost identical to the Muratorian Canon which, it has been suggested, might have been a Latin translation of his work.[19] As with all other church leaders, Hippolytus accepted only the four Gospels as records of the life and ministry of Christ, thirteen letters of Paul, Acts and 1 Peter and 1 and 2 John and the Apocalypse of John. He often quoted from Hebrews, though did not equate it with Scripture. There is little doubt that those books he did accept were placed on the same level with Old Testament texts. He quoted from other books, Hermas and *Didache* for example, but never with the same authority as the canonical literature which he introduced by such expressions as 'the Lord says' and 'the apostle says'. He was aware of 2 Peter, though did not recognize it as Scripture.

Clement of Alexandria (AD 153–216)—for more information on Clement see chapter 4

Clement arrived in Alexandria around AD 180 and ten years later was leader of the theological training school there until he was forced into exile under the severe persecution of the Emperor Severus. By 216 Clement was dead. He was a powerful and skilful warrior against the Gnostics. In his lengthy and detailed writings, he quoted from the New Testament books almost twice as often as from the Old Testament, and according to one source his total number of references to the Gospels and Paul amount to the staggering almost 3,000.[20] He is perhaps the first to refer to 'the New Testament', a phrase that he uses deliberately. Writing on faith Clement referred to 'the precepts both of the Old and of the New Testament'.[21] Some consider Tertullian was the first to use this designation,[22] but at least it shows that the phrase was now becoming familiar, and it must imply a certain body of known books.

Clement quoted from all the New Testament books with the exception of Philemon, James, 2 Peter and 2 and 3 John. However, as so often has to be said, the silence on a particular book cannot necessarily be taken as anything more than that the writer had no need to quote from it. In his *Exhortation to the Heathen* he quotes from Matthew, Romans, Corinthians, Galatians, Ephesians, Hebrews and Timothy.

Clement accepted only the four Gospels and insisted that they were entirely in harmony with each other. He was aware of a few other gospels, but he was careful always to distinguish them from the four and clearly never allowed them the same authority. Clement was prepared to use the title 'Scripture' when quoting from the Gospels; for example Matthew 23:37: 'The Scripture testifies: "As a hen gathers her chickens under her wings." Thus are we the Lord's chickens; the Word thus marvellously and mystically describing the simplicity of childhood.'[23]

Whilst Clement is hesitant on some New Testament books, his 'canon' was fairly well defined in his own mind. In a beautiful turn of phrase he united the Old and New Testament books in a vivid musical metaphor, 'the ecclesiastical symphony at once of the law and the prophets, and the apostles along with the Gospel'.[24] He also believed that Paul wrote Hebrews.[25]

Of particular interest is the testimony of Eusebius to the work of Clement. Eusebius claimed that Clement was using all the New Testament books 'without omitting the disputed books' — which may imply that Clement sat a little loosely to the idea of a canon of authoritative books. He appears also to have included Barnabas and the so-called Revelation of Peter among these.

Origen of Alexandria (AD 180–253)

Almost certainly a student of Clement, and as a theologian and biblical scholar, Origen towered above most of his contemporaries. One professor of New Testament Greek, Alexander Souter, referred to him, perhaps somewhat over generously, as 'the greatest biblical scholar who ever lived'.[26] Born in Egypt around AD 180 Origen later travelled widely as a teacher before, at the young age of eighteen, he succeeded Clement as head of the catechetical (training) school in Alexandria. For twelve years he worked hard and successfully until the bitter persecution under Caracalla forced him into temporary exile at Caesarea before he returned to Alexandria.

Sadly, unnecessary church wrangling over his ordination forced him back to Caesarea where he opened a new school which was even more successful than that at Alexandria. In

AD 250 under the persecution of Decius, he was tortured and condemned. Only the death of the emperor saved him from burning; however, his health had been broken and Origen died soon after in AD 253.

As a skilful biblical expositor, it is claimed that he expounded almost all the books of the Old and New Testaments. Although much of his work is lost, there is still a valuable collection.

Origen had travelled widely in Egypt, Arabia, Asia Minor, Greece, Rome and Palestine, and therefore he knew exactly which books of the New Testament canon were accepted by which churches. No one in his day had a more accurate knowledge of this subject.

Origen followed Clement in referring to 'the New Testament' and unequivocally identified them with the Old Testament books:

> This just and good God, the Father of our Lord Jesus Christ, Himself gave the law and the prophets, and the Gospels, being also the God of the apostles and of the Old and New Testaments.[27]

Origen reflected the views of the churches when he wrote:

> The records of the Gospels [he was referring to our four] are oracles of the Lord, pure oracles as silver purified seven times in the fire... They [the Scriptures] breathe the Spirit of fullness and there is nothing, whether in the Law or in the Prophets, in the Evangelists [the Gospels] or in the Apostles, which does not descend from the fullness of the Divine Majesty.

Origen had no doubt that the writings of the apostles were 'Scripture'. After quoting at length from Romans, for example, he continued: 'You will find also innumerable other passages in holy Scripture.'[28] He went further, and reflected the view 'throughout the churches' when he wrote of the Scriptures, both Old and New Testaments, as inspired by the Spirit:

> [The] Spirit inspired each one of the saints, whether prophets or apostles; and that there was not one Spirit in the men of the old dispensation, and another in those who were inspired at the advent of Christ, is most clearly taught throughout the Churches... Those Scriptures alone which were inspired by the Holy Spirit, i.e. the Gospels and Epistles, and the law and the prophets, according to the declaration of Christ Himself.[29]

Origen maintained that the four Gospels were 'the only indisputable ones in the church of God under heaven', and he went on to list some of the false gospels that are rejected, admitting that he had read them all to check their value.[30]

He admitted that Peter's second epistle is disputed by some, and a few even tried to reject Paul's second letter to Timothy 'but they were not able'. He had no doubt that Luke wrote both the Gospel and Acts, and that John wrote both his Gospel and the Apocalypse. Hebrews, from which he quoted on more than two hundred occasions, he attributed to the apostle Paul, though admitting that its authorship is uncertain: 'Who wrote the epistle, in truth, God knows.'

Having said this, Origen occasionally quoted from other, non-canonical books, though without attributing the same authority to them. He quoted from Clement of Rome, the Epistle of Barnabas, and the Shepherd of Hermas — which he even once suggests might be 'divinely inspired'. However, none of this detracts from the fact that it was only 'canonical' books that formed the basis of his many expository addresses. The only New Testament books that Origen did not use in his writings are 2 Peter and 2 and 3 John; he acknowledged that these, together with James, Jude and Hebrews, are disputed by some churches, but he did not share these doubts.

In a later work, written around AD 240, Origen summarized all twenty-seven books of the New Testament canon in a graphic style. The four Gospels:

> ...each gave forth a strain on their priestly trumpets. Peter, moreover, sounds with the two trumpets of his epistles ... Last of all thundering on the fourteen trumpets of his epistles he [Paul] threw down, even to their very foundations, the walls of Jericho, that is to say, all the instruments of idolatry and the dogmas of the philosophers.[31]

Eusebius of Caesarea (AD 260–340)

Eusebius was born around AD 260 and lived to his eighties. He was the first church historian, leader in the church at Caesarea from AD 313 and a close advisor to the Emperor Constantine after Constantine's acceptance of the Christian faith. By this time a library of Christian writings of significant historical value had been gathered at Caesarea, and Eusebius was able to make full use of it. His *Ecclesiastical History* (from Christ to AD 313) is one of the most valuable books from that period, since Eusebius had read many authors and had also travelled widely.

Eusebius claimed that he had enquired into the view of all the churches concerning the accepted books of Scripture, and he had searched widely.[32] There is no evidence that he was acting on the instructions of a church, council or the Emperor. His research was the result of his personal desire to discover the truth. He admitted that there was no one official list of canonical books, so he made his own from what books the various churches were using.

Why 27?

Eusebius drew up three lists:

- *The recognized books*: those universally accepted by the churches. Under this category Eusebius listed the four Gospels, Acts, the fourteen letters of Paul (including Hebrews), 1 Peter, 1 John and the Apocalypse of John — that is, twenty-two books that the churches accepted without question. Eusebius does, however, acknowledge that some disputed the authorship, though not the authority, of Hebrews.[33]
- *The disputed books*: those that most accepted and others queried or rejected. These were James, Jude, 2 Peter and 2 and 3 John, though they are known to most of the churches — the implication of this being that some churches simply may not have yet received copies of these books.
- *The rejected books*: those that all churches considered spurious and these included the Acts of Paul, the Shepherd of Hermas, the Acts of Peter, the Apocalypse of Peter, the Epistle of Barnabas, and the Gospel According to the Hebrews. These were the heretical or pseudepigraphal writings. Even worse than these books, in the mind of Eusebius, are such heretical books that pretend to come from an apostle such as the Gospels of Peter, Thomas, Matthias and others.

Given the widespread and independent nature of the churches and the heavy hand of persecution that frequently robbed the churches of their leaders, the catalogue of Eusebius showed a remarkable degree of unanimity.

For his own part, Eusebius accepted all except James, 2 Peter and Jude, though he admitted that they were widely used among the churches.

His list is not quite as tidy as the foregoing appears, because occasionally he placed the same book in two lists.

The Apocalypse of John is a case in point. However, Metzger provides a reasonable explanation for this in that Eusebius as the historian acknowledged that it was widely accepted among the churches, but for his own part he was exasperated by the extravagant use some were making of it and thus questioned its validity.[34]

Intriguingly, in AD 332 Eusebius was ordered by the Emperor Constantine to prepare fifty expertly inscribed copies of the Scriptures at the imperial expense. Eusebius carried out his orders and the books were presented with due ceremony to the Emperor for safe keeping. Since none of these books has yet been identified, we do not know what canon was included in that New Testament. Some think that *Codex Sinaiticus* and/or *Codex Vaticanus* (see chapter 9) may have been among those fifty copies. This is impossible to judge now, but they are both of the same time as Eusebius and their canon of books is identical to ours, with the addition of Barnabas and Hermas tacked on at the end of *Sinaiticus*; however, Eusebius rejected both of these.

There can be little reasonable doubt that by this time — early in the fourth century — the canon was almost universally fixed. Westcott concludes also, with only a little exaggeration, that the apocryphal writings 'had passed almost out of notice'.[35]

Athanasius of Alexandria (AD 296–373)

Athanasius was undoubtedly the most well-known theologian of the fourth century. Born around AD 296 he was educated in his home city of Alexandria, and at the Council of Nicea in AD 325 Athanasius took a leading role in the battle against Arius who denied the true deity of Christ. Soon after accepting leadership of the church at Alexandria, he took advantage of his position to set out the acknowledged limits of the New Testament canon.

In his *Festal Epistle* for the year 367 he listed the entire canon, both Old and New Testaments, exactly as we have it today (though Esther is missing from the Old Testament list but added as a useful book). The order of books varies, and Hebrews comes before 1 Timothy — evidence that Athanasius believed Hebrews belonged to Paul. Athanasius therefore offers us the first list of New Testament books exactly as we have them — the few doubts of Eusebius are evidently not shared by Athanasius. This is particularly significant because of the many apocryphal books that were circulating among the Egyptians who seemed to have a special fondness for heretical works.

Here are his own words:

> As the heretics are quoting apocryphal writings, an evil which was rife even as early as when St. Luke wrote his gospel, therefore I have thought good to set forth clearly what books have been received by us through tradition as belonging to the Canon, and which we believe to be divine. [Then follows the books of the Old Testament with the unusual addition of the Epistle of Baruch]. Of the New Testament these are the books ... [then follows the twenty-seven books of our New Testament, and no more]... These are the fountains of salvation, that whoever thirsts, may be satisfied by the eloquence which is in them. In them alone is set forth the doctrine of piety. Let no one add to them, nor take anything from them.[36]

Athanasius was the first to use the word 'canon' to refer to the collection of New Testament books, adding for further accuracy:

...that there are certain other books, not edited in the Canon, but established by the Fathers, to be read by those who have just come to us and wish to be instructed in the doctrine of piety. The *Wisdom of Solomon*, the *Wisdom of Sirach*, *Esther*, *Judith*, *Tobit*, the *Doctrine of the Apostles* [*The Didache*] and the *Pastor* [*Hermas*]. And let none of the apocrypha of the heretics be read among you.

Jerome (AD 347–420) and Augustine (AD 354–430)

If we could stop with Athanasius, the picture would be neat and complete. However, the history of the canon does not quite end there in the year AD 367. Various leaders from different parts of the rapidly crumbing Roman Empire revealed the extent of their own canon: Gregory of Nazianzus, Amphilochius of Iconium, Didymus the Blind in Alexandria, Epiphanius of Salamis (Cyprus), John Chrysostom in Antioch and later Constantinople (perhaps the first to use the word 'Bible' to refer to the complete collection of Old and New Testaments), Theodore of Mopsuestia (Cilicia) and Theodoret of Cyrrhus.

There are differences to a small extent between them, but it can be concluded that among them all, the canonical books as we know them were universally accepted and on only five books were any serious questions raised: 2 Peter, 2 and 3 John, Jude and Revelation — the latter, largely because of the abuse made from it by the millenarians, with their extreme views of the second coming.[37]

The position in the western churches is not too dissimilar. There are eccentricities to be sure, but the general pattern is clear, and Tyrannius Rufinus, who was born in AD 345, well reflects the churches in the West. His canon was the same as that of Athanasius (except that the order differed) and he listed additional books that were useful but not canonical, and those 'that should not be read out in church'.

Jerome (Eusebius Hieronymus), born around the same time as Rufinus, adopted the same canon for his famous Latin 'Vulgate', as did Augustine who was only ten years younger than Jerome. Whilst Jerome himself entertained no clear doubts about the twenty-seven books, he fairly listed the queries raised by some parts of the church. He was probably the first to suggest, in defence of 2 Peter, that the difference in style and Greek usage was probably due to different scribes who, at Peter's dictation, converted his Galilean Aramaic into Greek.[38] For Jerome, F. F. Bruce comments, the canon was fixed and 'to be received gratefully, preserved faithfully, and handed on intact'.[39]

Augustine was present at the Synods of Hippo (AD 393) and Carthage (397 and again in 419) at which the canon of twenty-seven books as we know them was recognized as the one in use universally among the western churches.[40] Whilst accepting the canon that he received, which was identical to that of Athanasius though with a slightly changed order, Augustine was not afraid to ask the pertinent question: 'Why these and no others?'

His answer was, like Jerome, not dependent solely on proving apostolic authorship. Instead:

- those with universal acceptance should be accepted without further judgement;
- those over which some churches expressed doubts should be accepted according to the majority of churches and the authority of their leaders.[41]

At this time, no council of leaders had attempted to pronounce on the canon on behalf of all the churches.

Inevitably, with Christian churches scattered well beyond the frontiers of the Roman Empire, and with no one church as 'supremo' above all the others, here and there the canon was ragged at the edges. But for all practical purposes, this marks the terminus of the debate on the canon of the New Testament, apart from the occasional maverick, until the time of the Reformation when Erasmus (a Roman Catholic) and Luther (a Protestant Reformer) made their own individual observations on canonical books over which they held personal doubts. Tyndale followed Luther in placing Hebrews (which Tyndale calls 'the epistle of Paul to the Hebrews'), James, Jude and Revelation at the close of the New Testament, but there is no evidence that either he or the English Reformers shared Luther's doubts.

The Peshitta in Syria

Sometime after AD 411, Bishop Rabbula of Edessa ordered a new translation of the Scriptures for the Syrian churches. Using the latest Greek manuscripts available, the Peshitta was widely used for a long time and fairly represented the canon used by the churches at Antioch and across Syria.[42] It did not contain 2 and 3 John, 2 Peter, Jude or the Apocalypse, but there were no 'rogue' entries either. From the numerous quotations in his extensive writings, it appears that John Chrysostom of Constantinople was using the same collection of books as the Peshitta. This is still the official canon of the Syrian Orthodox Church.[43]

Church councils

When the Emperor Constantine summoned the first ecumenical council at Nicaea in AD 325, we may well lament the fact that in all their deliberations they did not leave us a final list of canonical books, even though the authority of the 'Scriptures' was often referred to. However, even this silence is instructive.

The big issue on the table at Nicaea was clearly not the content of the canon, it was the true deity of Christ. Had the canon been an issue for debate, we can be sure that it would have been debated. Constantine appears to have been quite ready to meddle in the theological and ecclesiastical matters that he barely understood, and if he had needed to pontificate on the contents of the 'Scriptures' he would have done so. The Scriptures were the source of authority in the debate and the one thing that the delegates did not argue about was what constituted Scripture.

The first undisputed reference to the canon from a council of leaders comes in AD 397 at the third Council of Carthage. The list is precisely as we know it, but just as important is the fact that the council was not inventing a new list, it was at pains to make clear that it is 'what we have received from our fathers'.

Heading the list is the injunction that:

It was resolved that nothing should be read in church under the name of the divine scriptures except the canonical writings.

It was allowed, however, to read the stories of the martyrs on their anniversaries.

At the close of his detailed investigation into the history of the canon of the New Testament, Westcott pointed to the unity of the books to each other, the evidence in favour of the acceptance of all the books which far exceeds that of any other piece of ancient literature, and concluded:

It appeals with universal power to the conscience of mankind — because the same Spirit in the Church ... has never failed to seek in it afresh guidance and strength.[44]

Persecution

Unsurprisingly the increasing pressure upon the churches by government persecution also had an influence on the formation of the canon. Bruce Metzger expresses this well:

When the imperial police knocked at the door and demanded of Christians that they surrender their sacred books, it became a matter of conscience in deciding whether one could hand over the Gospel of John as well as, say, the Gospel of Thomas without incurring the guilt of sacrilege.[45]

According to Eusebius, on 23 February 303 under the Emperor Diocletian '...royal edicts were published everywhere, commanding that the churches be levelled to the ground and the Scriptures be destroyed by fire.'[46] It is unlikely that the Roman inquisitors could distinguish between Scriptures and other Christian literature, nor did they probably care, but it mattered to the Christians. It was a thorough search, as records of the time reveal, and at least three brave women were burned alive for refusing to hand over their sacred parchments. Few would pay the ultimate penalty unless they had good reason to believe that the 'parchments' were not less than the Scriptures.

Others, however, devised a sneaky way out. Caecilian, the Bishop of Carthage, hid his Scriptures and offered the writings of heretics instead! Those who handed over their scriptures were branded as *traditores* (those who surrender) by many in the churches. This led directly to a great division among the churches. In AD 312 the church at Carthage rejected Caecilian for this act of treachery and elected Donatus instead, who promptly disciplined the *traditores*. The Donatists considered themselves the pure church and, in the time of Constantine, rejected any interference of the state in church affairs; the schism rumbled on for almost two hundred years.

Persecution had some effect, though not a decisive influence, on sharpening the line between canonical and other literature.

Summary from AD 180

- Among all the church leaders from AD 180 onwards, without any exception beyond the cults, the four Gospels, Acts and thirteen letters of Paul were accepted without question. No other gospels were ever considered and almost the only time any others were mentioned was to reject them.
- 2 and 3 John, James and Jude and Hebrews were less quoted by the early leaders, but this does not mean they were not known. Their content was less relevant to the themes needed for the churches.
- The Apocalypse (Revelation) of John was quoted frequently by Irenaeus and Tertullian before the close of the second century; the only doubts expressed by some were because of the bizarre interpretations made by a few extremists.
- The single book over which there was significant doubt among the churches was 2 Peter, mainly because its style was considered to be very different from 1 Peter (which no one doubted was from Peter).
- No other books seriously jockeyed for a place in the canon.

The growth of the canon

- With the exceptions noted above, from the time of the apostles to Athanasius (AD 367), we have a united testimony for a consistent acceptance of New Testament books (and only those) from many leaders as far apart as (in today's terms): Israel (Caesarea), Syria (Antioch), Turkey (Smyrna), Greece (Corinth), Italy (Rome), France (Lyon), Tunisia (Carthage) and Egypt (Alexandria). The clear consensus by men of the calibre of Irenaeus (Europe) and Tertullian (Africa) proves that agreement on the New Testament books had been widespread for some time before AD 180 since the body of accepted books could not have appeared suddenly.

- Before the close of the third century, both Tertullian of Carthage and Clement of Alexandria were referring to the 'canonical' books as 'the New Testament'. The contents of the canon were by now assumed rather than debated. Only 2 Peter lacks a clear acceptance.

- By the middle of the fourth century Eusebius and Athanasius provide the clearest evidence of an agreed list of canonical books. That of Athanasius is identical to ours.

- Although no council of bishops had yet pronounced on the canon of the New Testament, by the time of Jerome and Augustine in the later fourth century it was considered to be fixed and agreed.

- Not until the Council at Carthage in AD 397 do we have an officially sanctioned list. Yet that list had been assumed by the majority of churches for more than one hundred and fifty years.

7. A library of lies

One of the greatest influences that forced the early church to identify the books of the New Testament canon was the spread of deviant cults in the first two centuries after the death and resurrection of Christ. The literature of these cults, more often than not claiming to be authentic sayings from the apostles, compelled the church leaders to establish the parameters for what properly belonged to the body of accepted literature — the New Testament canon.

There were too many groups for comfort. In fact the existence of a whole raft of false teachers, like Marcion, Valentinus, Basilides, Montanus and the rest, led to a strong and spirited defence of the truth by some of the most able literary leaders in the churches, among them: Justin, Ignatius, Irenaeus, Tertullian, Cyprian, Hippolytus, Clement of Alexandria, Origen and later Eusebius and Athanasius. However, it also led to some less wise men arguing from a self-defeating stand. Gaius in Rome spent some time trying to deny the authenticity of the Gospel of John in order to deny its use to the Montanists who were misinterpreting it. As Bruce comments, 'an excessive price to pay for the maintenance of catholic orthodoxy'.[1]

A library of lies

'Some mighty fiction'

Circulating within the first two centuries after the death and resurrection of Christ, there were scores of documents, letters and gospels, some claiming to come from the pen of the apostles themselves. These are known as 'pseudepigrapha', which means 'false writing', and the false gospels are often referred to as 'apocryphal gospels'. Even during the lifetime of Paul he warned the churches 'not to become easily unsettled or alarmed by some prophecy, report or letter supposed to have come from us' (2 Thessalonians 2:2). For this reason the apostle frequently drew attention to his own signature at the close of his letters (1 Corinthians 16:21; Galatians 6:11; Colossians 4:18; 2 Thessalonians 3:17; Philemon 19).

However, in all this literature there is very little additional information concerning the life of Christ. The so-called 'gospels' are not really gospels at all since they contain almost no history. The Infancy Gospel of Thomas offers to fill in the lack of information in our Gospels on the childhood of Jesus; there are absurd accounts of the subsequent life and death of Pilate, and even a History of Joseph the Carpenter — probably written to support the later view that Mary was a perpetual virgin — but there is little else by way of 'history'. Most of the Gnostic writings are no more than isolated sayings attributed to Jesus or his followers. The Gnostics were not interested in doctrine or absolute statements of theology, they preferred to express their religion in obscure statements and visionary insights which, in reality, few could understand.

Fortunately, as we have seen in previous chapters, the church was not without its strong defenders of the truth. Two of the most able were Irenaeus of Lyons and Tertullian of Carthage. In his work *Against Heresies* Irenaeus was well acquainted with the false writings circulating in his day and he summarized the authors: 'Every one of them generates something new day by day, according to his ability; for no one is deemed "perfect", who does not develop among them some mighty fiction.'[2] Irenaeus analysed in detail the various forms of Gnostic heresy and revealed their absurd interpretation of Scripture texts. However, almost in despair at their ever-changing views, he added:

> But since they differ so widely among themselves both as respects doctrine and tradition, and since those of them who are recognized as being most modern make it their effort daily to invent some new opinion, and to bring out what no one ever before thought of, it is a difficult matter to describe all their opinions.[3]

Far away from Gaul (France), the scene of Irenaeus' labours, an even more formidable lawyer was soon to drive his skilful pen into the heresy of Marcion. Tertullian also wrote against Valentinus and Praxeas. He referred to the wealthy shipowner Marcion as 'O shipmaster of Pontus'[4] and went on to mock his picking and choosing from the Gospels and apostles: '…so I should be glad if you would inform us under what bill of lading you admitted the Apostle Paul on board.'

Tertullian dispensed with the false Acts of Paul and Thecla with the explanation that 'in Asia, the presbyter who composed that writing, as if he were augmenting Paul's fame from his own store, after being convicted, and confessing that he had done it from love of Paul, was removed from his office'.[5]

He complained that some, like Marcion, mutilated the text by selecting only what they wanted, whilst others, like Valentinus, perverted the text by twisting its meaning. The church leaders were well able to recognize the heretics; as the Muratorian Canon had observed: 'It is not suitable for gall to be mingled with honey.'[6]

Marcion

In July AD 144, the wealthy shipowner from Pontus on the Black Sea was on trial for heresy before the leaders of the church in Rome. Marcion had arrived from Asia, where his extreme views had been rejected, and he made a generous donation to the church funds at Rome. Marcion believed passionately Paul's doctrine of justification by faith, to the extent that he rejected the Old Testament altogether, believing it to be the product of an evil god, a demiurge. The old and new covenants were, according to Marcion, irreconcilable. He also believed that all the apostles had misunderstood Christ as the Jewish Messiah and therefore he accepted only Luke's Gospel and ten of Paul's letters — and even these he severely edited, pruning Luke into what is possibly the Gospel of the Lord (see pages 145-6).[7]

But Marcion also held Gnostic beliefs, and for all this he was tried, found guilty and his liberal monetary gift was handed back. The shipping magnate went off to spread his heresy elsewhere and started his own church.

The story was passed round the churches that on one occasion Marcion met the strong defender of the truth, Polycarp, who was soon to be burnt by the Romans for his faith. 'Recognize us, Polycarp,' urged Marcion. To which Polycarp responded, 'Yes indeed, I recognize the firstborn of Satan.'[8]

Polycarp was not the only one to abhor Marcion. Justin Martyr, when writing his defence of the Christians to the Emperor Titus, tore into this arch heretic:

The devils put forward Marcion of Pontus, who is even now teaching men to deny that God is the maker of all things in heaven and on earth, and that the Christ predicted by the prophets is His Son, and preaches another god besides the Creator of all, and likewise another son. [9]

Unfortunately the edited canon of Marcion became widespread in the second century, especially in the West. But the fact that he could pick and choose from the books that were generally accepted is clear evidence of a firming up of the canon prior to Marcion in the mid second century. Bruce concludes: '…it can be argued with some show of reason that Marcion's "canon" was his revision of an existing collection of New Testament writings.'[10] And Metzger rightly claims: 'It is nearer to the truth to regard Marcion's canon as accelerating the process of fixing the Church's canon, a process that had already begun in the first half of the second century.'[11] However, from the material that is available, Marcion has the dubious honour of being the first to leave us a canon of New Testament books — unfortunately his was an emasculated one.

The Gnostics

Salvation for the Gnostics — and scholars debate how much of a Gnostic Marcion was — became a matter of personal enlightenment or knowledge of the secret mysteries revealed in their own writings. *Gnosis* is a Greek word for knowledge. All Gnostics followed Marcion's dismissal of the Old Testament and its god and believed that the natural, physical world was evil, because it had been created by an evil god; thus it was opposed to the spiritual world. This was a religious dualism that led them to despise the material life and encouraged some, like the followers of Carpocrates and his son Epiphanes, to practise some rather sordid rites. However, not all Gnostics used their beliefs as a licence for licentiousness, though all considered that salvation was through self-enlightenment and freeing oneself from the prison house of the soul — the body.

The Gnostics believed that Jesus was the one to give this enlightenment, but their Jesus was very different from the man portrayed in the four New Testament Gospels. Most of them believed that the Christ only *seemed* to be a real man — a view known as Docetism from the Greek verb *dokein* 'to seem'; and that the Christ was substituted by another — many Gnostics believed Simon of Cyrene — at the cross. This led to endless tales of Jesus visiting other lands, marrying Mary Magdalene and so forth.

Against Heresies by Irenaeus is a masterly demolition of the novelties of Gnosticism that reveals the author was thoroughly acquainted with the contemporary writings and well equipped to respond. He was not alone in asserting that the Gnostics could find no support for their views in the four Gospels, the Acts of the Apostles and the letters of Paul — and the Gnostics admitted this. Their response was twofold: on the one hand, they selected from the accepted books only those that they wished to use (as Marcion did); whilst on the other hand, they claimed that the real message had been communicated secretly to the disciples (or some of them at least) and thus they could produce their own 'gospels' to reveal the secrets.

Irenaeus confirmed the widespread acceptance of the four Gospels by showing how even the heretics used and abused them:

So firm is the ground upon which these Gospels rest, that the very heretics themselves bear witness to them, and, starting from these, each one of them endeavours to establish his own peculiar doctrine.[12]

Tertullian complained in the same way:

They actually treat of the Scriptures and recommend (their opinions) out of the Scriptures! To be sure they do. From what other source could they derive arguments concerning the things of the faith, except from the records of the faith?[13]

Valentinus was another influential Gnostic leader, a native of Alexandria and contemporary of Marcion, who made use of the Gospel of Truth, which came to light among the Nag Hammadi texts that will be considered in the next chapter. Valentinus often quoted from some of the books of the New Testament, though he twisted the texts with his own fanciful interpretations; a point which both Tertullian and Irenaeus were quick to recognize.[14]

Tertullian contrasted the methods of Marcion and Valentinus. Whereas Marcion used the knife to cut out passages he did not agree with, Valentinus simply twisted the meaning of Scripture to suit his own ends:

He took away more, and added more, by removing the proper meaning of every particular word, and adding fantastic arrangements of things which have no real existence.[15]

In addition to Marcion and Valentinus, Irenaeus singled out Basilides for a swingeing attack.[16] Basilides from Alexandria, perhaps the most able and certainly the most literary of the Gnostics, produced twenty-four books to expound Gnostic views; Irenaeus understandably calls it 'an immense development to his doctrines'.[17] Only fragments of these remain today, but clearly they were widely read and persuasive of many during the second century. Basilides presents an unholy mixture of Greek mythology and twisted gospel narrative which included the 'fact' that Simon of Cyrene was crucified in place of Jesus who, meanwhile, 'received the form of Simon, and, standing by, laughed at them'.[18]

Irenaeus also targeted Carpocrates who headed up a sect of Gnostics who believed Jesus was little more than any other man.[19] Possibly the Secret Gospel of Mark (see page 145) was in the preserve of the Carpocratians, and Clement of Alexandria hints at their sordid nocturnal rites, whilst Irenaeus does much more than hint:

> They practise also magical arts and incantations; philtres [a drink to inflame the passions] and love-potions; and have recourse to familiar spirits, dream-sending demons, and other abominations.[20]

Significantly, when Irenaeus condemned the Marcosians (another breed of Gnostics from Marcus, a disciple of Valentinus) he specifically castigated them for inventing 'an unspeakable number of apocryphal and spurious writings, which they themselves have forged, to bewilder the minds of foolish men, and of such as are ignorant of the Scriptures of truth', and went on to refer to false statements that we can find in the Gospel of Truth.[21]

It is out of these Gnostic stables that most of the false writings of the first few centuries came. Sadly, it was the Gnostic writings that influenced the first understanding of the Christian gospel by Islam in the seventh century, and today the Koran perpetuates the long discredited stories put around by the Gnostics.[22]

The Gospel of Judas — 'a fictitious history'

The Gospel of Judas was launched into the world by the *National Geographic* magazine in April 2006, with dire predictions that this revelation 'could create a crisis of faith'. Others suggested that we may have to rethink the story of Christ in the light of this new revelation.

The only thing that is new about the fragmentary text of this ancient piece of literature is that for the first time in eighteen hundred years we can read it. The original was probably written just prior to AD 180 because in that year Irenaeus referred to a 'Gospel of Judas' in his treatise *Against Heresies*. Irenaeus claimed that he had gathered together much of the heretical writings so that he would be better able to respond to them. At this point he was writing against a sect he referred to as 'Cainites', an unorthodox group clearly out of step with the mainline views of the churches — see Jude 11 in the New Testament.

Here are the precise words of Irenaeus:

> They declare that Judas the traitor was thoroughly acquainted with these things, and that he alone, knowing the truth as no others did, accomplished the mystery of the betrayal; by him all things, both earthly and heavenly, were thus thrown into confusion. They produce a fictitious history of this kind, which they style the Gospel of Judas.[23]

That is virtually all that was known about this 'gospel' until a tattered fragment of it was discovered in Egypt in 1978 and came into the hands of a group of interested experts in 1999. The fragment, written in Egyptian Coptic on thirteen pieces of papyrus, took five years to reassemble, decipher and translate because of its very poor condition; about fifteen per cent has been irretrievably destroyed. It takes about ten minutes to read it through. The papyrus is reliably dated between AD 220 and 340, so it is a copy made at least half a century after the original.

In brief, the Gospel of Judas tells the 'secret account of the revelation that Jesus spoke in conversation with Judas Iscariot during a week three days before he celebrated Passover'.[24] It recounts the following story.

The disciples were offering a prayer of thanksgiving before a meal; Jesus laughed at them, chiding them that they were under the impression that 'your god [will be] praised' — a clear Gnostic view that the god of the Old Testament was an inferior god. The disciples became angry and 'began blaspheming against him in their hearts'. When challenged by Jesus, only Judas could claim to know who he really was. Jesus took Judas on one side and shared with him some of 'the mysteries of the kingdom'. Later Jesus interpreted a dream of the disciples, though much of this is either obscure or missing from the fragment; what is clear, however, is that Jesus accused them of worshipping the god of the Old Testament and of leading the people astray.

Subsequently Judas shared privately with Jesus that he had had a vision of all the disciples stoning him, and in response Jesus told him more of the 'mysteries' of the kingdom, promising that 'You will be cursed by other generations — and you will come to rule over them. In the last days they will curse your ascent to the holy [generation].' Jesus then shared with Judas things that no eye had ever seen. What follows is an obscure speech — not helped by the fact that large parts are missing — about the origin and destination of the world, all in Gnostic language.

The critical phrase

In the final part of the conversation, Judas asked about the future of those who have been baptized in his name, to which Jesus replied: 'But you will exceed all of them. For you will sacrifice the man that clothes me.'

That is the critical phrase. The Gospel of Judas has been hailed as revealing that Jesus effectively asked Judas to betray him, and that therefore Judas was in reality not a traitor but a hero carrying out the orders of Christ. That phrase is the sole authority for such a claim.

The Gospel of Judas is certainly the text that Irenaeus referred to around AD 180 since it contains all the hallmarks of the Gnosticism that he was writing against.

- The fact that Jesus mocked the disciples for praying to the god of the Old Testament is in line with the Gnostic view that the Old Testament god was a demiurge, inferior to the God of the New Testament and opposed to him.
- It is clearly a Gnostic writing since it contains a reference to 'Sophia'. She was the goddess of wisdom whose offspring was identified with the god of the Old Testament; she was loved by the Gnostics and is frequently referred to in Irenaeus' critique of Gnosticism.[25]
- The reference to 'the man that clothes me' reveals the Gnostic view that the Christ merely inhabited the body of a man and left before the crucifixion.
- The esoteric language throughout is typical of all Gnostic writings.

It is not difficult to understand why the Gospel of Judas disappeared under the sand sometime in the third or fourth centuries and resurfaced in a single papyrus almost destroyed beyond recognition, nearly two millennia later. It did not merit a place in anyone's library — it still does not.

Fancy that! — more from the libraries of lies

Apart from the Gospel of Judas, and the Gnostic documents discovered in 1945 that we will look at in the next chapter, there is little that has come to light recently that was not well known, and well written about, in the nineteenth century. These tattered fragments that have created such a stir in recent days can be added to the collection whose contents was known, examined and dismissed as false one hundred and fifty years ago.

We have evidence of some fourteen false gospels available today (including the Gospel of Judas), though numbers will vary depending upon how the documents are classified. However, in case anyone should wonder if this does not, after all, cast doubt upon the four Gospels as the only claimant to 'canonicity' consider these facts about the pseudo gospels:

- All were written much later than the four Gospels and could not have been written by or with the direction of an apostle.
- Not one was ever a contender for a place in the canon of the New Testament.
- Each of them betrays itself by its content (for example, the historical inaccuracies in the Gospel of Peter and the Gnostic tendencies in the Gospel of the Lord).
- Some are mere fragments (for example, the Gospel of Bartholomew).
- Others are known only by name since we do not possess a copy (for example, the Secret Gospel of Mark).
- Not one is a full story from the birth to the ascension of Christ as we have in the four canonical Gospels.

Of the items at our disposal, I have selected a few that fairly represent the whole.

The Infancy Gospel of Thomas

The earliest of the existing manuscripts for the Infancy Gospel of Thomas (which is not to be confused with the Gospel of

141

Thomas, part of the Nag Hammadi Library) goes back to the sixth century; although Irenaeus refers to two stories that are in fact found in this pseudo gospel, so it may have been written in the middle of the second century. It does nothing more than fill in the gap of the life of Christ up to the age of twelve. The book begins: 'The stories of Thomas the Israelite, the philosopher, concerning the works of the childhood of the Lord.'[26]

Among the novel inventions of the writer, at the age of five Jesus fashioned twelve sparrows out of clay which, when he clapped his hands, they flew away. However, it is immediately followed by the account of a young lad who, having spoiled one of Jesus' miracles, was punished by Jesus and he promptly 'withered up wholly'. Another lad bumped into him and was immediately struck dead. Others who admonished him, including his teachers, were struck with blindness or otherwise punished. Hardly a propitious start for the Prince of Peace!

More positively, the prodigious wisdom of Jesus amazed his teachers, and he was able to heal and even to raise the dead, including one of his playmates after a fatal fall. The account closes with the story of Jesus being left behind in Jerusalem, recorded in Luke 2:42–52. Apart from a few harmless additions to that story, the account is so similar in detail to Luke's that it is almost certain that the author had access to the Gospel. With this single exception, it is not difficult to see why the early church would have rejected the highly imaginative stories contained in this brief pseudo gospel; they are so contrary to the character of Christ revealed in the Gospels and betray the foolish desire of men to fill in where God has chosen to be silent.

The Arabic Gospel of the Infancy

This fills in the details of what happened when the family fled to Egypt. It is doubtful whether it was written much earlier

than the eighth century, but clearly its intent was to exalt
Mary who is the means of a number of miracles. The family
even meet the two thieves whom the Christ child prophesies
would later be crucified with him — and we have their names:
Titus and Dumachus! Having returned to Bethlehem, Jesus,
at the age of seven, makes animals and birds of clay that then
walk and fly. Here and there some phrases show acquaintance
with the Gospels.

The Gospel of Pseudo-Matthew

Two documents are involved here, both from the fifth century.
The main document *claims* to be from Jerome (AD 347–420)
whose translation of the Bible into Latin became the official
version for the Roman Catholic Church. The Gospel of
Pseudo-Matthew begins: 'The Book of the Birth of the Blessed
Mary and of the Infancy of the Saviour. Written in Hebrew by
the Blessed Evangelist Matthew, and translated into Latin by
the Blessed Presbyter Jerome.'[27]

Mary is presented to us as a perfect child — her story begins
at the age of three years — who received her food from the
angels who talked often with her. She determined to remain
a virgin all her life and eventually was committed to the
care of Joseph, along with five other virgins. Mary becomes
pregnant by the Holy Spirit and, with many embellishments,
the story runs more or less parallel to the Gospels at this
point. Significantly Luke 2:1–2 is quoted exactly but then the
nativity is filled out with many imaginary details. The story
clearly reflects the widespread view in the fifth century of
the perpetual virginity of Mary; and a few miracles are added
to prove it. The story continues through the circumcision
of the child, the visit of the Magi, the slaughter of the boys
in Bethlehem by Herod and the flight to Egypt. On the way
even lions and leopards adored him 'showing subjection by

wagging their tails'. Various miracles follow, including the idols of Egypt falling down. From here we are taken to the childhood of Jesus and some of the stories reflect those in the Infancy Gospel of Thomas.

Whilst it is clear that the writer was acquainted with the four Gospels, and at times can even quote from them, he never acknowledges his source.

The Gospel of Peter

This short and incomplete account was discovered in the Egyptian desert by a French archaeologist around 1886. It was a copy (possibly in the seventh to ninth centuries) of an original that may have been written in the middle of the second century. It begins with the trial of Jesus, and our confidence in it as a historical document is immediately destroyed since it assumes that Herod was responsible for the crucifixion of Jesus and when Joseph of Arimathea, 'the friend of Pilate', requested the body from the governor, Pilate had to ask Herod for it! Since only the Roman Governor had the authority to pronounce and carry out the death sentence, this immediately betrays the late date of writing and the author's ignorance.

This may be one of the Gnostic writings since it questions the reality of the suffering of Christ, though that is debated. There are sufficient similarities to the Gospels to suggest the author had some knowledge of them, and the added details, in the light of the opening historical gaffe, need not be taken too seriously. The centurion given charge of the tomb is named as Petronius, and he pitched a tent for his men, kept guard, and saw bizarre visions of Jesus and the angels.

The story now switches to Mary Magdalene and the women who came to the tomb; this part follows fairly closely the Gospel records. Peter then takes up the story from his own perspective, admitting that the disciples were all afraid and, without any reference to the appearances of Jesus in Jerusalem, concludes: 'But I, Simon Peter, and my brother Andrew, having taken our nets, went off to the sea. And there was with us Levi of Alphaeus whom the Lord...'[28] Here the account ends abruptly and the rest is lost.

The Gospel of Peter is irrelevant as a document to throw any new light on the trial and death of Christ and, once again, it is not difficult to appreciate why it was rejected by the early church as spurious. It certainly was not Peter who wrote it, but it is typical of the pseudepigraphal documents.

The Secret Gospel of Mark

A letter was discovered in 1958 that appears to be from Clement of Alexandria to someone named Theodore. In it he refers to a secret Gospel according to Mark held by the church in Alexandria. Clement is clearly dismissive of it and reveals the attitude of the church leaders to these pseudo gospels:

> Now of the things they keep saying about the divinely inspired Gospel according to Mark, some are altogether falsifications, and others, even if they do contain some true elements, nevertheless are not reported truly. For the true things being mixed with inventions, are falsified, so that, as the saying goes, even the salt loses its savour.

The Gospel of the Lord

This document begins: 'The written account of the life of Jesus Christ, preserved in its original Greek by Marcion, son of Philologus, bishop of Sinope. 130 anno domine, Rome.'[29]

Marcion was the Gnostic leader who extracted selective portions from the New Testament, and this is largely a synopsis of Luke's Gospel, often verbatim, with little added though much taken away; what we have closes long before the crucifixion. The date of AD 130 makes it much later than the four Gospels to which Marcion clearly had access.

Filling the gaps

For contenders to be included among the four Gospels, there is nothing better to offer than the above. However, just as we saw with the Infancy Gospels, there was an insatiable desire to fill the gaps in our knowledge by letters also. Thus, in the fourth century someone kindly invented an Epistle to the Laodiceans to fulfil Colossians 4:16. Others provided letters written by Paul, Peter, Herod, Pilate, Joseph of Arimathea, the woman healed of an issue of blood (Matthew 9:20–22), and even Jesus himself. We also have a little correspondence between Paul and Seneca — the Roman philosopher and Nero's tutor!

In all, there are some sixty documents that make up what is known as the New Testament pseudepigrapha. Many of the details in them are hopelessly inaccurate, as for example when the forger of the Letter of Herod obviously forgot that the Herod of the time of our Lord's birth was not the same man as the Herod of his trial and crucifixion! Among other false writings are the Preaching of Peter, the Acts of Peter, and the Apocalypse of Peter.

- These are all so different from the true letters of Peter that the early church leaders had no hesitation in rejecting them.
- Not one of them appears in the lists of books used as Scripture by the early churches.

- All were written far too late to have come from the hand of an apostle.

It would be tedious to examine them all, so two small examples will suffice.

The History of Joseph the Carpenter

First published in 1722 it is thought to have originated in Coptic sometime in the fourth century, though some place it much later. Cowper claims that the story 'is characterised by features by no means devoid of interest, although most improbable, unreasonable, and in the worst possible taste'.[30] This latter comment presumably alludes to the fact that, unlike other false writings, this one actually claims to have been related by Jesus himself. Referring to Mary he asserts: 'I loved her with a peculiar affection, with the good pleasure of my Father, and the counsel of the Holy Spirit; and I was incarnate of her, by a mystery surpassing the capacity of the reason of creatures.'[31]

Apart from a few historical blunders, in the story Joseph was widowed with a family before he married Mary who then bore the Christ as her only child; it is therefore not hard to discover one reason why it was written, since from this story alone, the Roman Catholic Church could cull the doctrine of the perpetual virginity of Mary. A large part of the story concerns the painful old age of Joseph until Christ gave him new health and he died at the age of 111 years.

The Epistle to the Laodiceans

The oldest copy known is dated AD 546, although it was mentioned by writers from the fourth century on. Pope Gregory the Great, who became Pope in AD 590, may have rescued it from oblivion, in which case he was especially gullible.

Clearly Paul's reference in Colossians 4:16 to a letter he had sent to the church at Laodicea was the cue for someone to make up a memo — for that is virtually all that it is — to fill the gap. Fortunately the anonymous forger was little gifted either in counterfeit or a knowledge of the apostolic mind. It consists of a few scattered sayings culled from Paul's genuine letters, adds nothing new at all, makes no mention of anyone by name in the entire letter — which would make it unique for Paul — and contains nothing to make it worthwhile the Colossians sending a messenger to Laodicea to collect a copy! It is hard to imagine how it would be possible to construct a less convincing forgery.

Admittedly some of the forgeries are more credible than this one, though none of them fooled the early church leaders.

Montanus and the Montanists

Although much of the early false writing was influenced by the Gnostic heresy, they were not the only bad guys around. The Montanists grew up in Phrygia in the middle of the second century and spread rapidly. The simplest way of describing their views is as an early form of extreme Pentecostalism. Believing and practising ecstatic experiences of the Holy Spirit and guided by revelations and prophecies, its leader, Montanus, spoke in tongues and claimed to be the Paraclete promised by Jesus (John 14:15–17 and 17:7–15). He was joined in his movement by two women, Prisca and Maximilla, who abandoned their husbands to follow Montanus. The utterances of the three of them, often speaking in the first person as God, were carefully recorded and given the status equal to that of the Hebrew Scriptures and the letters of the apostles. By the turn of the second century, one of the church's great leaders, Tertullian, had joined their ranks.

The influence of the Montanists on the development of the canon of the New Testament was both negative and positive. Negatively they were producing their own 'scriptures' as a result of the prophecies, and this confused the issue; one writer claimed an infinite number,[32] though significantly none has survived. In addition, the heavy emphasis on the end of the world, and the extravagant language used, caused some of the churches to react against the Apocalypse of John and, because of the use the Montanists made of it, the epistle to the Hebrews also.

Positively, however, the extravagancies of Montanism forced the church to begin to settle the issue of the authoritative apostolic Scriptures. By the end of the first century the Montanists had been denounced as a heretical sect and one writer, in condemning them, claimed that his hesitation before was that he did not wish to be seen 'to add or detract from the doctrines or precepts of the Gospel of the New Testament, which it is impossible for one who has chosen to live according to the Gospel, either to increase or to diminish'.[33] Clearly this writer towards the end of the second century was well aware of a standard of 'Gospel' books.

'Old falsehoods have been preferred to older truths'

There is no evidence that the pseudepigrapha were circulating widely in the first three centuries of the life of the Christian church. The Muratorian Canon was adamant that 'it is not suitable for gall to be mingled with honey', and early in the fourth century Eusebius had little difficulty listing those books that were to be decidedly rejected. It was only later that they came back into vogue.

Of course parts of the church across the empire and beyond accepted some of the apocryphal works as 'canonical' for a while, but that no more tells us what the vast majority of churches believed than to assume that the views of modern-day cults tell us what the Christian churches today believe. It is also true that very occasionally some of the early church leaders themselves made allusions to apocryphal writings, though they never referred to them with the authority they gave to the New Testament books.[34] A few scattered weeds do not describe a field.

The Middle Ages saw a revival of interest in the apocryphal documents and some were useful to bolster — perhaps were even written for — the creeping errors of the Roman Catholic Church. Certainly, for example, the History of Joseph the Carpenter supports the doctrine of the perpetual virginity of Mary. Many of the apocryphal stories found their way into the Morality and Miracle plays that were so popular in the Middle Ages, and into art, the Roman Catholic breviary, and later into our Christmas carols as well — since the ox and the ass adoring the infant Christ is taken directly from the Gospel of Pseudo-Matthew.[35] An adaptation of the Infancy Gospel of Thomas even found its way into Icelandic legends, and it is a tragic matter of history that in the seventh century Mohammed was more familiar with the apocryphal gospels than the four New Testament Gospels.[36]

Sadly, 'Old falsehoods have been preferred to older truths.'[37]

The ring of truth is missing

Those who are well read in the books of the New Testament will have little difficulty recognizing the wholly different genre of the apocryphal gospels. C. S. Lewis made this point well when he commented that such a reader would find himself saying, 'No, it's a fine saying, but not his. That wasn't how he talked.'[38]

Significantly, not one of the existing documents sets out to deny any of the history that is written in the four Gospels; apparently the best they can hope to achieve is to add to them. As Bruce Metzger points out, some set out to supplement and others to supplant the four Gospels.[39] But their attempts are poor: the 'ring of truth' is missing, the historical context (such as there is) is often inaccurate, the additional sayings of Jesus are mostly either unintelligible or irrelevant, and the miracles are often frivolous. Metzger, a usually cautious and restrained scholar, comments: 'One can appreciate the character of the canonical Gospels and the near banality of most of the gospels dating from the second and third centuries.'[40]

Besides all this, most of the texts are incomplete fragments, and the reason for this is obvious: they were bypassed by the churches as unreliable and, falling into disuse, eventually disappeared. Their chief value is to reveal, by contrast, the beauty, simplicity and integrity of the New Testament Gospels.

B. W. Cowper, an eminent scholar writing long before the more recent discovery of Gnostic documents, commented on the added stories in the false writings:

> No difficulty stood in the way; ancient documents could easily be appealed to without necessarily existing; spirits could be summoned from the other world by a stroke of the pen, and be made to say anything; sacred names could be written and made a passport to fictions, and so on *ad libitum*.[41]

That well sums up the pseudepigrapha of the first two or three centuries in the story of the canon of the New Testament.

Explaining the fiction

Much of the strange and mischievous philosophy of the
Gnostics that twisted many of the fundamental doctrines of
the Christian faith, including the creation of the world, the
origin of evil, the fall of the human race, the true deity of
Christ and his work of atonement, can be dismissed as the
plaything of natural pride and the love of 'secrets'.

However, perhaps there is a human side to the invention
of some of those additional stories of the life of Christ. The
four Gospels admittedly leave gaps at the very point where
we would love to know more. What happened to the family
in Egypt? What more could we know of the childhood and
youth of Jesus? And since we have only one thousandth part
of the work and teaching of Christ over three years of public
ministry, there is much more that could have been told — as
the apostle John himself admitted (John 20:31–31; 21:25).
The temptation has always been to fill in the gaps.

In the mid nineteenth century, Dr Charles Ellicott
commented on the apocryphal gospels: 'We know before we
read them that they are weak, silly and profitless — that they
are despicable monuments even of religious fiction — yet
still the secret conviction buoys us up, that perchance they
may contain a few traces of time-honoured traditions.'[42] It
is this longing to know what God has not chosen to reveal,
an unwillingness to accept that there are 'secret things [that]
belong to the Lord our God' (Deuteronomy 29:29), that has
driven many to add where they had no business to.

During the latter part of the second century and well into
the third, the church leaders were engaged in a long battle
against those who dismissed the accepted authority of the
growing body of New Testament books and wrote their own
instead. The church needed to establish the truth both in
doctrinal terms and in the accepted books of Scripture.

Summary

- In the first two centuries of their existence the churches were assailed by many heretics who produced their own fictitious writing, but they were opposed by a wise and capable body of church leaders.
- The apocryphal books, like the Gospel of Judas, so popular today, were known and rejected before the close of the second century by the churches whose leaders mounted a robust challenge against the heretics.
- The library of the Gnostics and others is a world of difference from the letters and works of the orthodox leaders, let alone the Scriptures themselves — and this was easily recognized because the ring of truth was absent.
- However, the fact that the leaders of heresies, like Marcion and Valentinus in the second century, selected some of the New Testament books and rejected others presupposes a known body of generally accepted Scripture.
- The earliest false writing is dated at least half a century after the last New Testament book was written.
- Those that claim to be 'apostolic' are poor forgeries invented to fill the gaps.

8. A bad read by the Nile

In the year that the Second World War drew to a close, and eighteen hundred years after Marcion was disciplined for heresy and Irenaeus had published his five-volume *Against Heresies*, an Arab peasant discovered under the sand on the east bank of the Nile in Upper Egypt a collection of old books. The spot was close to a small town called Nag Hammadi and the find, which is now known as the Nag Hammadi Library, consisted of sixty-one fragments covering fifty-two separate documents in thirteen codices (books). They had been written some time in the fifth century, though they are considered to be copies of earlier works from possibly the third century. They were written not in Aramaic or Greek, but in Coptic, an old Egyptian language written mostly with Greek characters. After a long and tortuous journey, during which they were split up and sold, all thirteen documents are now in the Coptic Museum in Old Cairo.

The Nag Hammadi Library

The Nag Hammadi Library was translated into English in 1977 and is important because we can now read, from their own writings, much more of the beliefs of the early Gnostics, whom we met in the previous chapter, than was possible before. The early church leaders who wrote against them are now seen to have given us an accurate assessment of Gnostic beliefs.

This collection has spawned any number of books, a film and a renewed debate about the four Gospels in the New Testament. Among the documents were the Gospel of Truth, the Gospel of Thomas, the Gospel of Philip, the Gospel of Mary (of Magdala), the Gospel of the Egyptians and the Apocryphon of James.

Since the evaluation of one scholar of most of the Gnostic writing is 'tedious and verbose',[1] in this chapter we will survey only a representative sample of the books from Nag Hammadi. Even those that claim to be 'gospels' are not gospels in the way we understand the word, since they contain almost no history. Although different strands of Gnosticism held differing views, Marcion fairly reflected their position in general.

For the most part we have only fragments or badly damaged copies, since they were never accepted by the church generally and therefore soon became lost to the world when the Gnostics largely died out by the sixth century. Irenaeus complained that: 'Every one of them generates ... day by day ... some mighty fiction'[2], and the literature of the Nag Hammadi Library is part of that 'mighty fiction'.

The Gospel of Truth

The Gospel of Truth is the fullest expression of the Gnostic mind of all the books in the Nag Hammadi Library and some believe that it is the work of the leading and influential Gnostic Valentinus, written around the middle of the second century. It reveals the Gnostic love of the obscure, and the expressions and thoughts are a world away from the records of the four Gospels. The theme is that ignorance of the Father is darkness and the darkness is dispelled only by attaining true knowledge of oneself and the world. This is classic Gnosticism.

As one's ignorance disappears when he gains knowledge, and as darkness disappears when light appears, so also incompleteness is eliminated by completeness. Certainly, from that moment on, form is no longer manifest, but will be dissolved in fusion with unity.[3]

In a passage that reflects the 'monism' of Gnostic thinking we have the heart of Gnostic philosophy — 'monism' is the denial of a distinction between matter and mind and a belief that all is one:

Since the perfection of the All is in the Father, it is necessary for the All to ascend to him. Therefore, if one has knowledge, he gets what belongs to him and draws it to himself. For he who is ignorant, is deficient, and it is a great deficiency, since he lacks that which will make him perfect. Since the perfection of the All is in the Father, it is necessary for the All to ascend to him and for each one to get the things which are his. He registered them first, having prepared them to be given to those who came from him.

This reference to 'the All' comes in frequently. In a passage that expresses the incarnation in a less than orthodox way, the Gospel of Truth also reveals the Gnostics' view of God as being both Father and Mother:

The logos of the Father goes forth into the All, being the fruit of his heart and expression of his will. It supports

the All. It chooses and also takes the form of the All,
purifying it, and causing it to return to the Father and to
the Mother, Jesus of the utmost sweetness.

The Gospel of Truth bears no resemblance whatever to the
New Testament record of salvation and presents a philosophy
that cannot be considered as Christian spirituality at all.

By AD 180 Irenaeus was aware of this so-called 'gospel'
since it had only just begun circulating when it came to his
attention:

Indeed, they have arrived at such a pitch of audacity, as
to entitle their comparatively recent writing *The Gospel
of Truth*, though it agrees in nothing with the Gospels of
the Apostles, so that they have really no Gospel which is
not full of blasphemy. For if what they have published is
the Gospel of truth, and yet is totally unlike those which
have been handed down to us from the apostles, any
who please may learn, as is shown from the Scriptures
themselves, that that which has been handed down from
the apostles can no longer be reckoned the Gospel of
truth.[4]

In other words, Irenaeus presented his readers with a stark
choice: they must accept either the so-called 'Gospel of Truth',
or the Gospels handed down from the apostles — both cannot
be true.

From the point of view of the canon, the significance of the
Gospel of Truth is the fact that it refers to most of the New
Testament books, especially the four Gospels, Paul's letters, Hebrews and Revelation, and treats them as inspired and authoritative. Since this false gospel was written around AD 140 it is
evident that well before that date the New Testament books
'must already have enjoyed authority for a considerable time'.[5]

The Gospel of Thomas

The Gospel of Thomas (which is not the same document as the Infancy Gospel of Thomas described in the previous chapter) is perhaps the most important of the Nag Hammadi documents. It contains one hundred and fourteen sayings, supposedly of Jesus, revealed to the apostle Thomas. Many of these bear similarities with the teaching of Jesus. Some are straightforward quotations which reveal a clear knowledge of the Gospels, as for example: 'Jesus said, "If a blind man leads a blind man, they will both fall into a pit"' (34) — compare Matthew 15:14 and Luke 6:39. Thirteen parables are included that, though much shorter in Thomas, are paralleled in the Gospels.

However, much else is vague and esoteric. Here is an example of a complete mishmash of hints from the teaching of Jesus and sayings that are obscure:

> Jesus said to them, 'If you fast, you will give rise to sin for yourselves; and if you pray, you will be condemned; and if you give alms, you will do harm to your spirits. When you go into any land and walk about in the districts, if they receive you, eat what they will set before you, and heal the sick among them. For what goes into your mouth will not defile you, but that which issues from your mouth — it is that which will defile you' (14).[6]

Of course, the whole point of the Gnostic writings was that only those given special illumination will understand the secrets and gain salvation. Salvation is from within: 'If you bring forth what is within you, what you bring forth will save you' (45).

It is claimed by some today that one reason why the Gnostic gospels were destroyed was because they revealed the 'true' story of the leadership of women in the first-century church. If this is so, what should we make of this?

> Simon Peter said to them, 'Let Mary leave us, for women are not worthy of Life.' Jesus said, 'I myself shall lead her in order to make her male, so that she too may become a living spirit resembling you males. For every woman who will make herself male will enter the Kingdom of Heaven' (114).

Here is another example of the esoteric in the Gnosticism of this false gospel:

> Jesus saw infants being suckled. He said to his disciples, 'These infants being suckled are like those who enter the kingdom.' They said to him, 'Shall we then, as children, enter the kingdom?' Jesus said to them, 'When you make the two one, and when you make the inside like the outside and the outside like the inside, and the above like the below, and when you make the male and the female one and the same, so that the male not be male nor the female female; and when you fashion eyes in the place of an eye, and a hand in place of a hand, and a foot in place of a foot, and a likeness in place of a likeness; then will you enter the kingdom' (22).

Irenaeus made no direct reference to the Gospel of Thomas, and since he was familiar with most of the Gnostic writings, it lays open the serious possibility that this one had not been written before AD 180 — long after the death of the apostles and the circulation of the four Gospels.

Notwithstanding the over-generous comment by Metzger that 'of all the tractates in the Nag Hammadi library [this] seems to be the closest to the New Testament',[7] it shows only how far removed from the canonical books all the others are.

The Gospel of Philip

The Gospel of Philip does not claim to be the teaching of Jesus, but is a handbook of Gnostic thinking, much of it obscure. Whatever one's view of this gospel, it is impossible to read it without appreciating the simplicity and clarity of the four New Testament Gospels by contrast. Here is a sample of its obscurity:

> Light and Darkness, life and death, right and left, are brothers of one another. They are inseparable. Because of this neither are the good good, nor evil evil, nor is life life, nor death death. For this reason each one will dissolve into its earliest origin. But those who are exalted above the world are indissoluble, eternal.[8]

Clearly this is the work of one who stood outside the mainstream of Christian teaching, because some of the expressions are heretical, for which the early church leaders rightly condemned them. As an example here is another passage in which the Gnostic denial of the Virgin Birth is apparent:

> Some said, 'Mary conceived by the Holy Spirit.' They are in error. They do not know what they are saying. When did a woman ever conceive by a woman? ... And the Lord would not have said, 'My Heavenly Father' unless he had had another father, but he would have said simply 'My father'.

A bad read by the Nile

According to this gospel, the world came about through a mistake:

> For he who created it wanted to create it imperishable and immortal. He fell short of attaining his desire. For the world never was imperishable, nor, for that matter, was he who made the world. For things are not imperishable, but sons are. Nothing will be able to receive imperishability if it does not first become a son. But he who has not the ability to receive, how much more will he be unable to give?[9]

It is hardly surprising that the early church leaders condemned this kind of teaching. It is the Gospel of Philip that introduces the relationship of Mary Magdalene with Jesus, and wildly extravagant claims are made suggesting that it reveals that Jesus and Mary were married. In fact it does nothing of the kind. There is not one word or phrase in any literature of the first four centuries that makes this claim.

There is certainly plenty of mystery about this apocryphal book, which is presumably what is intended. However, one thing is clear, the writer was acquainted with some of the New Testament and there are at least ten direct quotations, some introduced by 'the word'. For example:

> 'That is why the Word says, "Already the axe is laid at the root of the trees"' (Matthew 3:10).

> 'The Word said, "If you know the truth, the truth will make you free"' (John 8:32).

All of this demonstrates that this part of the Nag Hammadi Library must have been written long after the New Testament was circulating in some form.

The Gospel of Mary

Much of this has been lost and it is hardly possible to assess what Mary is really supposed to have said because large sections are missing. Early small fragments of the text in Greek were available before the Coptic Nag Hammadi discovery, but there are significant differences between the Greek fragments and the longer Hammadi Coptic text. Barely a thousand words survive. As with the Gospel of Philip, it is misleading to refer to it as a 'gospel' since we learn nothing about the life of Christ. What we have here is the mystic teaching attributed to Mary Magdalene. After the ascension of Christ, the disciples were in despair and it was Mary who roused them to action and courage. Let the text speak for itself:

> Then Mary stood up, greeted them all, and said to her brethren, 'Do not weep and do not grieve nor be irresolute, for His grace will be entirely with you and will protect you. But rather, let us praise His greatness, for He has prepared us and made us into Men.' When Mary said this, she turned their hearts to the Good, and they began to discuss the words of the Saviour. Peter said to Mary, 'Sister, we know that the Saviour loved you more than the rest of woman. Tell us the words of the Saviour which you remember which you know, but we do not, nor have we heard them.' Mary answered and said, 'What is hidden from you I will proclaim to you.'[10]

Mary then delivered the secret things that she had learned from Jesus. The little we have does not advance our understanding much apart from confirming the mysteries of Gnosticism. The book presents Mary Magdalene as a favourite of Jesus and one who possessed a knowledge and spirituality

superior to that of the apostles. Nothing more is said about
her relationship to Jesus than is recorded above.

The Gospel of the Egyptians

Without question the most bizarre of all the documents in
the Hammadi Library is the Gospel of the Egyptians. Some
of the early church leaders were aware of it, and Clement
of Alexandria referred to it, but all rejected it entirely as
spurious. Large sections are missing, but even if they were not,
it would little advance our understanding of the strange book.
It is not a 'gospel' in any sense and has virtually nothing to do
with the Christian story or the Christian religion, giving the
impression more of the ramblings of a deranged mind than a
serious attempt at religious writing.

Written by 'Eugnostos the beloved' (whoever he was), it
claims to be 'The Holy Book of the Great Invisible Spirit',
and is full of pretended symbol and unintelligible language.
Two specimens, typical of the entire document, will suffice to
refute the wild suggestions of some writers that these 'gospels'
were possible alternatives to the four in the New Testament.

> Three powers came forth from him; they are the Father,
> the Mother, (and) the Son, from the living silence, what
> came forth from the incorruptible Father. These came
> forth from the silence of the unknown Father.[11]

Later, the name of the 'Father of Light' is offered in the
strange formulae of seven vowels each reproduced twenty-
two times:

> Domedon Doxomedon came forth, the aeon of the
> aeons, and the throne which is in him, and the powers

which surround him, the glories and the incorruptions. The Father of the great light who came forth from the silence, he is the great Doxomedon-aeon, in which the thrice-male child rests. And the throne of his glory was established in it, this one on which his unrevealable name is inscribed, on the tablet [...] one is the word, the Father of the light of everything, he who came forth from the silence, while he rests in the silence, he whose name is in an invisible symbol. A hidden, invisible mystery came forth:

iiiiiiiiiiiiiiiiiiiiii   EEEEEEEEEEEEEEEEEEEEE
o o o o o o o o o o o o o o o o o o o o o o o o
u u u u u u u u u u u u u u u u u u u u u u u u
eeeeeeeeeeeeeeeeeeeeee   aaaaaaaaaaaaaaaaaaaaaaa
OOOOOOOOOOOOOOOOOOOOOOOOO

That, to all commentators, remains 'a hidden, invisible mystery'!

With thought and imagination, the reader may find some connection in what follows with the first chapter of John's Gospel!

The great Logos, the divine Autogenes, and the incorruptible man Adamas gave praise, (and) they asked for a power and eternal strength for the Autogenes, for the completion of the four aeons, in order that, through them, there may appear [...] the glory and the power of the invisible Father of the holy men of the great light which will come to the world, which is the image of the night. The incorruptible man Adamas asked for them a son out of himself, in order that he (the son) may become father of the immovable, incorruptible race, so that, through it (the race), the silence and the voice may appear, and, through it, the dead aeon may raise itself, so that it may dissolve.

If the Gospel of the Egyptians is typical of the religion of those who gathered the original collection and hid them on the banks of the Nile, it is not difficult to see why Irenaeus, Tertullian and others of the early church leaders were so strident in their rejection of this wacky philosophy. It is equally hardly surprising that such material was lost beneath the sands of Egypt for eighteen hundred years. It was rubbish then, it is still rubbish today.

The *Apocryphon* of James

These claim to be secret revelations to James, the brother of Jesus, and to Peter. They are in the form of a conversation between Jesus and his disciples and apparently these are things that Jesus 'did not wish to tell to all of us, his twelve disciples'; though why, is hard to imagine since, even if the sayings here are true, they are hardly such as should be kept secret. The *Apocryphon* does not quote from the Gospels, but shows familiarity with the parables in them. There are a few new parables and new supposed sayings of Jesus. The *Apocryphon* is at variance with the Gospels in claiming that Jesus remained with his disciples for eighteen days after his resurrection. It adds nothing to our certain knowledge of Christ and his teaching, and nothing to our knowledge of the Gnostics either. We may well question whether Jesus would ever have said, either openly or in secret, 'The Father has no need of me, for a father does not need a son, but it is the son who needs the father, though I go to him. For the Father of the Son has no need of you.'[12]

This, of course, betrays the Gnostic view of Christ as being little more than a great man.

'Falsely called knowledge'

The Gnostics had been around for a long time, and there is evidence that some of the letters of the apostles were intended to undermine their deviant doctrine. Paul warned Timothy about 'opposing ideas of what is falsely called knowledge' (1 Timothy 6:20), and similarly set the Colossians on their guard against 'hollow and deceptive philosophy' and those whose 'unspiritual mind puffs him up with idle notions' (Colossians 2:8,18). When Paul prayed that the Colossians might 'be filled with a knowledge of his will, through all spiritual wisdom and understanding', he was perhaps deliberately using the very words so central to Gnostic philosophy: *knowledge, wisdom, understanding.*

John equally laid emphasis upon the true light and truth and testing the spirits (1 John 1:5–7; 4:1–3). Similarly the errors denounced by Peter (2 Peter 2) and Jude (vv. 8–16) fit the beliefs of the Ophites, a sect of the Gnostics known also as Cainites. According to Irenaeus of Lyons, the false Gospel of Judas came from this stable.[13]

Since the discovery of the Nag Hammadi Library in 1945 we can see just how confused and vague their teachings were. The total of all pseudepigrapha does not exceed sixty documents. Only a few of them claim to be 'gospels' and five of those are in the collection found at Nag Hammadi; these 'gospels' are mostly fragments, not one recounts the story of the adult life of Christ, and all were clearly rejected by the early church. The very fact that much of the false writing pretended to come from the apostles at least proves that the test of apostolic authorship was considered essential to qualify for recognition as part of Scripture.

Inevitably all these bits and pieces that have come to light in recent years have kept historians in business and some, against all reason and good scholarship, have suggested that in these we have the original stories! However, even if we put them all together, we could certainly not make a coherent record of the life and teaching of Christ such as we have in any one of the four Gospels. The Gnostic writings bear no comparison with the simple and straightforward teaching of the four, nor were they meant to, because only the enlightened could gain salvation through the knowledge of the mysteries.

F. F. Bruce aptly summarizes the use of these books from the Nile:

> Private enterprise will provide editions of the gospels which include one or more of the Nag Hammadi documents along with some or all of the canonical gospels; or compilers of gospel harmonies or synopses will produce handbooks in which passages ... are presented in parallel columns with comparable passages from the New Testament books. These works may be useful to the student; they are irrelevant to the question of the canon.[14]

The contents of these writings that were excluded from the canon easily betray why they were not accepted. We can now read some of the Gnostic writings for ourselves and judge how meaningless they often are. Similarly, they are in such obvious contrast to the New Testament Gospels and letters that we have little difficulty in realizing why the early church leaders rejected them.

Since the great champions of the early church were clear and detailed in their criticism of these false gospels and their cultic authors, it must be insisted that no one should read the pseudo writings of the Nag Hammadi Library and allow themselves to be influenced by them, without first reading Irenaeus and Tertullian in their works against the heresies.

Summary

- The Gnostics and other erroneous groups were using most of the canonical New Testament books as authoritative before the middle of the second century; it is therefore a given that such books were already widely accepted and circulating as Scripture.
- The false gospels and letters betrayed themselves by their late date of composition — well beyond the time of the apostles — and by their teaching which clearly conflicted with the canonical books and the accepted doctrines of the churches.
- Although the earliest Gnostic writings are dated to the middle of the second century, almost one hundred years after the New Testament was complete, many of them carry apostolic pseudonyms i.e. pretending to be apostolic.
- Around sixty apocryphal documents are available today; most are incomplete and many are mere fragments.
- No more than a dozen of this total claim to be gospels, five of which are in the Nag Hammadi collection. These contain little or no true history, and no coherent record of the life and teaching of Jesus Christ could be compiled from them.
- The leaders of the churches across the empire had no difficulty in distinguishing 'the gall from the honey'.

9. Where are the manuscripts?

A nyone interested in the subject of the canon of the New Testament is bound to ask, sooner or later: 'How old are the earliest manuscripts of the New Testament that we possess?' That's a fair question, and the answer will certainly throw up some interesting surprises.

There are three main sources for our information about the development of a canon of the New Testament:

- The writings of the church leaders which reveal what books they were acquainted with and how they viewed them. This was our subject in chapters 5 and 6.
- The age of existing Greek texts of New Testament books. This will be covered in this chapter and the next.
- The earliest translations of the New Testament into other languages, known as 'versions'. We will briefly look at this subject later in this chapter.

Papyrus and parchment

What materials were used for recording the Christian Gospels and letters? Many of our earliest Greek manuscripts of New

Testament books were written on papyrus, made from the pith of the papyrus plant that grew abundantly by the River Nile. Strips of papyrus would be laid vertically and then another layer placed horizontally across them; the whole was then pressed hard, dried in the sun and rubbed smooth. Papyrus was in use at least 3,000 years before the church was born. It was cheap but flimsy, and easily destroyed by strong sunlight or damp.

Another name for papyrus was *biblos,* and a *biblion* was a roll of *biblos*; hence our word 'Bible' which literally means 'books'. Papyrus could be rolled into a scroll, some of which reached thirty-five feet, and occasionally more. Generally it was only written on the side where the horizontal strips had been laid, and in narrow columns, two columns to a page being the most common.

A far more durable material for writing on was leather (often referred to as 'parchment'). This came from the skins of sheep, goats or cattle and was not only strong and long-lasting, but it was pliable so that it could be rolled and unrolled with less danger of cracking. 'Vellum' was a high quality leather made from calf-skin: although the young of sheep, goats or deer were also used to produce vellum.

Scrolls and codices

Whilst scrolls were at first the common form of storing writing, most of our Greek manuscripts are in the form of books or codices (singular: codex), a word which comes from the Latin word *caudex,* a tablet. The lengthy scrolls were overtaken by codices, by which a large sheet of parchment or papyrus was folded and (sometimes) stitched together. Thus a scroll of thirty feet or more (required for the Gospel of Luke), which was both clumsy and time-consuming to roll and unroll, was replaced by a book. This more easily fixed the contents, and many more documents could be bound together.

Jewish literature was written on parchment scrolls, pagan literature on papyrus scrolls, whilst the Christians preferred papyrus codices. Of all the New Testament papyri so far discovered, less than a handful are from scrolls. Clearly the Christians preferred to use codices since it was cheaper (because both sides of the paper was used), easier to store, and more simple to locate a particular section than having to unroll a scroll. The Gospel of Luke would require thirty-two feet of scroll, and the entire New Testament would be some two hundred feet in length.[1]

It is obvious that a scroll of the entire New Testament would be impossible, and up to AD 300 it would be most unlikely for the entire canon to be contained within one codex because of the expense and bulk. Thus the books circulated in clusters, beginning with the Gospels and followed by the apostle Paul and then Acts and the other letters, concluding with the Revelation of John.

At the same time, on the basis that 'it is not suitable for gall to be mingled with honey', it would require some thought and decision as to which books would be bound together. We would expect this to have had a significant influence on the clarity of the canon of the New Testament. All four Gospels or all the letters of Paul could be bound together in one book, which was impossible with a scroll. There is good reason to believe that just as the Reformers were quick to take advantage of the printing press in order to speed the distribution of the newly translated New Testament from the Greek, so the Christians in the first century were among the first to see the potential of the idea of binding parchment into a book.

So, what is available and how old is it?

Uncials

The 'uncials', or 'majuscules', were written in a style that can best be described as what we know as capital letters. Each letter was separated from its neighbour and the text had all the appearance of clean dignity and careful scribal copying. All works of literature were written in uncial because it was the style of the scholar. Generally our oldest texts are the uncials, and therefore we do not have so many of them. Just under three hundred of the available texts are in the uncial form. Naturally these carefully scribed and separated letters took up a lot of space when both papyrus and parchment were scarce and expensive, and they also took more time and care to copy. Of the uncial codices available we shall later mention just four of the most valuable.

Cursives and minuscules

By the latter part of the first century, two developments made the distribution of writings more accessible, just as the invention of printing furthered the spread of the Bible in the sixteenth century. The large uncial, capital letters of the Greek alphabet was reduced to cursive, or joined-up writing. By far the majority of the available material was in the form of Greek cursives. This made the whole document smaller, which saved space and therefore paper. Cursive was at first used mainly for ordinary, everyday communication and often common words were abbreviated.

Cursives were attractive for those who wanted copies of the Scriptures both fast and cheap. Inevitably, care in transmission was sometimes more lax, and with the use of abbreviations and a running script it was easy for a careless copier to slip here and there. However, it must be emphasized that, with rare exceptions, these errors are small and easy to correct from the great number of texts available.

A development of the cursive style was the 'minuscule' writing which, as the word implies, meant that the letters were much smaller even than cursive. But this style was not adopted until sometime in the ninth century AD and therefore their evidence is of no help to us in tracing the early history of the progress of the canon.

To avoid confusion and to simplify, we will add the cursives and minuscules together under the one heading of cursive. To date there are fifty-eight cursives of the complete New Testament, and thousands more of parts from fragments to almost whole books. In total there are just over 2,800 cursives. Some go back to the third or fourth centuries, although most of this material comes between the ninth and fifteenth centuries.

Autographs and copying

Everyone accepts that we do not possess any document that we can say is the 'autograph' — that is, from the actual hand of an apostle. All that we have are copies of copies. This does not make them less valuable, because the same is true of all ancient literature. For those who may be afraid that this allows for thousands of errors to creep in during the process of copying, we can respond that since there are literally thousands of copies available, the overwhelming agreement among them offers reassurance of the accuracy of the transmission.

For a collection of books as popular and well used as the New Testament, we would not expect to find many very early complete manuscripts. The New Testament books were not museum exhibits or collectors items; on the contrary, they were in regular use — and for the first two hundred and fifty years they were circulating during times of severe persecution when it was common for the books, and sometimes their owners, to be burnt.

Although it is not our subject here, it is worth making a passing comment on the issue of copying. The popular assumption is that during the course of copying the texts of the New Testament a multitude of errors have crept in until it is almost impossible to know what the original autographs may have said. The problem with this statement is that the first part is true, but the conclusion is nonsense!

No other collection of ancient literature presents so many copies for the experts to examine. With around 5,500 Greek manuscripts of all or parts of the New Testament available, there is no one New Testament book that is not backed by scores of available texts copied over a few hundred years. There are, in fact, many discrepancies, but they are almost all in the realm of minor differences in a single, similar word or letter.

Here is just one example: at 1 John 1:4 we have a difference between 'our joy' and 'your joy'. The difference in the Greek is as close as it is in the English — just one letter. A scribe copying from dictation might hear it incorrectly or, in the afternoon weariness of a hard day scribing, his hand might inadvertently pen the wrong word. The difference is minimal. When people talk and write about 'thousands of errors' this is the level of the vast majority, though they rarely know this. The availability of so many texts generally enables the scholar to determine what the true text ought to be.

B. F. Westcott, whose skill as a New Testament textual critic is still recognized after one hundred and fifty years, claimed that even these differences did not amount to more than a 'thousandth part' of the whole New Testament. Another scholar has commented: 'There is no body of ancient literature in the world which enjoys such a wealth of good textual attestation as the New Testament.'[2] More recently, Bruce Metzger, a cautious scholar of the New Testament text, after outlining some of the inevitable errors that do creep in after centuries of copying, adds this important caveat:

> Lest the foregoing examples of alterations should give the impression that scribes were altogether wilful and capricious in transmitting ancient copies of the New Testament, it ought to be noted that other evidence points to the careful and painstaking work on the part of many faithful copyists. There are, for example, instances of difficult readings which have been transmitted with scrupulous fidelity.[3]

He then provides a few examples where an obvious grammatical blunder has been faithfully transcribed by a copyist who would not dare to change the text in front of him and concludes: 'These examples of dogged fidelity on the part of scribes could be multiplied.'

Incidentally, the cost of professional copying would have been prohibitive for most Christian congregations. Late in the third century, Emperor Diocletian fixed the price of scribal work at a minimum of 20 denarii for 100 lines (*stichoi* as they were known). According to Matthew 20:2 a denarius would be the daily pay for a common labourer. On this basis the Gospel of Luke would have cost around three months wages for a professional scribe to copy. Some of the more literate church members doubtless copied for free![4]

How old are the manuscripts?

This is not strictly our subject here because the age and quality of the earliest Greek manuscripts that are available for our

New Testament text is another question altogether. However, it may be worth establishing a level playing field as an example of the way people, sometimes academics among them, set up one rule for the New Testament and quite another for other literature of a similar period. Before the close of this chapter we will have seen that our earliest complete New Testament in a single volume can be dated to AD 350, some portions of the New Testament go back to AD 200 and fragments to AD 100 and earlier. Does that seem long distant from the autographs?

Then let's take a few examples of well-known and well-used literature from approximately the same period.

Josephus

Josephus was a Jewish scholar who wrote his *Jewish Antiquities* (History of the Jews) in AD 93/94. Thus, for practical purposes he was a contemporary of the apostles. His work is used and quoted regularly as a valuable source for the history of the Jews from creation to the fall of Jerusalem. What we are never told is that whilst there are available scores of fragments, large and small, plus incomplete sections, the earliest complete text of all twenty chapters is not until the fifteenth century! The earliest manuscripts of the first ten books are dated to the ninth century and for the last ten books the eleventh century.[5] The oldest text of any work of Josephus (and it is not from the *Antiquities*) is a single fragment that goes back to the third century.[6]

Tacitus

Tacitus was the Roman historian who lived between AD 55–120. All that is now available of his work are his *Annals*, which covered the history of Augustus to Nero, and his *Historiae*, which is the history of the Roman Empire from AD 69–97. It is believed that he originally wrote his history in thirty books, but only because of a reference by Jerome in the fourth century. The first six books of his *Annals* survive in a single manuscript (*Codex Mediceus*) to be found in the Laurentian library in Florence and dated AD 850; books 11–16 and his *Historiae* are, again, preserved in a single copy dated in the fifth century. This is an important history, referred to often, yet the only source for much of it is a single manuscript copied almost eight hundred years after the original.[7] To be fair, there is also evidence from the fifth and sixth centuries of writers quoting from the work of Tacitus.

Julius Caesar

Julius Caesar wrote his own account of his campaigns in Gaul (France), which is known as the *Gallic Wars*. Allowing for his own bias for his personal glory, the record is nevertheless considered by all historians to be a valuable and authentic window into a crucial period in the career of Caesar and the development of the Roman Empire. It certainly portrays Caesar as one of the great military commanders of all time. The campaigns in Gaul covered the years 58 to 55 BC. The oldest existing manuscript of Caesar's *Gallic Wars* was copied nine hundred years after his death. There are many manuscripts available for the *Gallic Wars*, 'but only nine or ten of them are considered good'. In fact scholars have the same fun with 'textual criticism', including a search for a common source, as they have with the New Testament. One even concedes that there are 'a considerable number of passages in which, though all the manuscripts agree, the text is obviously wrong'![8]

To summarize the comparison of these three texts with that of the New Testament:

The earliest complete New Testament in one volume with all the twenty-seven books:	300 years after the death of the apostles.
The earliest complete text of Josephus' *Antiquities*:	1300 years after the death of the author.
The earliest complete text of Tacitus' *Annals*:	800 years after the death of the author.
The earliest complete text of Caesar's *Gallic Wars*:	900 years after the death of the author.

But this does not tell the whole story. Allowing for inevitable errors in copying, in order to arrive at an accurate text we need a large number of available early texts to compare. Against the, literally, thousands of part manuscripts that we possess of the New Testament, there are relatively few of all the others.

How many texts are available?

The material available for establishing the best text for our New Testament is enormous — far more than for any other piece of literature up until the modern age of printing. But the subject of this book is concerned not with establishing the best text, but surveying how and when the New Testament books came to be accepted into the canon. There are around 5,500 Greek manuscripts containing all or part of the New Testament and therefore in what follows we will single out only a handful of the most significant that will aid us in our search.

Greek papyrus

These are the manuscripts written on papyrus, and as well as their common name indicating who discovered them or purchased them, they are all given a code number beginning with the letter P. In what follows it will be noted that there are no papyrus records of a complete New Testament. This is not surprising since, as we have seen, a complete New Testament was bulky, expensive and time-consuming to copy. Thus smaller collections would often be preferred. The significance is not what is missing, but what is included.

1. The Chester Beatty Papyri — P45, P46

Between 1930 and 1931, the well-known collector Chester Beatty purchased some papyri which consisted of parts of the Old and New Testaments and the Apocrypha, the book of Enoch and a treatise by the second-century leader, Melito of Sardis. Later, more sections were purchased by Beatty and the University of Michigan, and both parties encouraged Sir Frederick Kenyon, one-time director of the British Museum, to publish the complete text. These collections do not all come from the same codex.

The most generally accepted dating for this collection is AD 200 or at the latest 250.[9] Whilst only fifteen of the New Testament books are represented, these papyri do show that by the middle of the third century collections were already circulating.

However, P46 is possibly the oldest surviving collection of Paul's letters (ten in this case), originally dated around AD 200 but redated in 1988 by Young-Kyu Kim to around AD 85.[10] The main objections to this early date are that it would be:

• The oldest surviving Christian manuscript.
• The oldest surviving papyrus codex.

- The oldest use of abbreviations for the sacred names (known as *nomina sacra*).

However, there is no reason, apart from assumptions, that it may not be all of these. The Chester Beatty Papyri are now in the Beatty Museum in Dublin.

2. *The John Rylands Papyrus — P52*

The John Rylands Papyrus is housed in the John Rylands University Library in Manchester, England. Acquired in 1920 by the papyrologist B. P. Grenfell, it is a tiny fragment (6 cm by 9 cm) and contains only five verses from John 18:31–33, 37–38. It is part of a codex because verses 37–38 are on the verso (reverse side). The fragment was dated around AD 125 by the papyrologist Colin Roberts, Fellow of St John's College, Oxford, when he published his findings in 1935. Some two decades later he and Ramón Roca-Puig increased this to later in the second century. This was the latest possible date, and it meant that within one hundred years of John's death, a copy of his Gospel was already circulating in Egypt — a long way from where John wrote it in Ephesus.

The date of P52 is still a matter of discussion. Some scholars are convinced that it can be placed as far back as around the year AD 100,[11] in which case, to quote an earlier John Rylands librarian, 'when the ink of the original autograph can hardly have been dry'.[12] Because of its clear similarities of style with P64 and P67 (see below), Carsten Thiede believes that P52 may be dated to before AD 70.[13]

Bruce Metzger helpfully concludes that had this little fragment been known during the middle of the nineteenth century, the liberal critics from Germany like Ferdinand Baur 'could not have argued that the Fourth Gospel was not composed until about the year 160'.[14] Unfortunately, many modern writers both of academic books and popular novels still seem to be unaware of this fact.

3. The Bodmer Papyri — P66

Martin Bodmer acquired this valuable document in Egypt in the 1950s. Among the papyri is an almost complete codex of John's Gospel, which is now held by the Bodmer Library of World Literature at Cologny, Geneva, and known as the Bodmer Papyrus II (P66), commonly dated to AD 200, but more recently to c. AD 125.[15] If this is so, we have the text of John's Gospel within possibly thirty years of his death! There are many alterations and corrections in P66 which implies that it was copied in haste.

4. The Bodmer Papyrus — P75

Dated between AD 175 and 225 this document contains almost the whole of Luke and John and is therefore the earliest example of an (almost) complete copy of Luke's Gospel, and one of the earliest of John. It is also in the Bodmer Library, and 102 pages of 144 have survived in carefully written uncial letters. This provides more clear evidence of the circulation of the Gospels before the close of the second century.

Other documents in this collection include portions of 1 and 2 Peter and Jude, Acts and Paul's epistles, but these are dated later in the third and fourth centuries.

Greek codices

We come now to the major collections of complete, or near complete, New Testaments. The fine condition and early date of these is strong evidence for the care with which collection of the canonical books were being gathered well before the end of the fourth century.

1. *Codex Sinaiticus*

This complete codex of the New Testament was discovered in 1859 at a monastery on Mount Sinai (hence its name) by Dr Constantin von Tischendorf of the University of Leipzig. It originally contained the whole Old Testament plus six books of the Apocrypha, though parts had been destroyed with age before the book was rescued. Apart from this, it is in excellent condition. *Sinaiticus* was originally copied in Alexandria, found its way to the monastery on Sinai, was sold to Alexander II, the Tsar of Russia, and purchased in 1933 from the communist authorities in the Soviet Union jointly by the British Government and the British Museum for £100,000. It is now in the British Library.

Sinaiticus is the only known complete copy of the New Testament in uncial script. As noted earlier in chapter 4 the Shepherd of Hermas and the Epistle of Barnabas are added at the end, separated from the canon. It is dated around the middle of the fourth century AD. That date is significant and it has given rise to the following possible association.

According to Eusebius, the church historian and spiritual advisor to the Emperor Constantine, around the year AD 331 the emperor ordered 'fifty copies of the sacred Scriptures' to be produced on fine parchment and with the utmost attention to accuracy. They were duly presented to him 'magnificently and elaborately bound'.[16] Some scholars have suggested that *Sinaiticus* may well have been one of those fifty Bibles. However, the addition of Hermas and Barnabas at the end makes this connection unlikely since Eusebius definitely listed those two as rejected books.

Whether or not this connection can be made, it is clear that by the middle of the fourth century there was sufficient universal agreement over the books of the Bible for Eusebius to have so many copies made.

2. Codex Vaticanus

This codex has been in the Vatican Library at Rome since before 1475, but even the Dutch scholar Erasmus was not allowed to use it when he was compiling the text for a Greek New Testament early in the sixteenth century. *Vaticanus* is also a possible contender for being one of those fifty copies ordered by Constantine. It contains both the Old Testament (together with most of the Apocrypha) and the New Testament in Greek, though the beginning and the end are missing. *Vaticanus* may be slightly older than Sinaiticus, earlier in the fourth century, and is considered by some scholars to be the best Greek text we have of the New Testament. Hebrews is placed among the letters of Paul. *Vaticanus* underlines the fact that, since a codex of this quality could hardly have come about in a vacuum, the completed canon of twenty-seven books must have been gathered at least late in the third century.

3. Codex Alexandrinus

Alexandrinus was presented to King Charles I of England by the Patriarch of Alexandria in 1627. Written somewhere between AD 350 and 450, it originally contained the whole Old and New Testaments (including the Apocrypha), though much for the New has been destroyed through age. The only 'rogue' books present are 1 and 2 Clement, which is odd since they were not in general use by this time. Like *Sinaiticus*, this is now in the British Library.

4. *Codex Ephraemi*

This is another fifth-century manuscript which contained the entire New Testament, though large parts, including 2 Thessalonians and 2 John, are now lost. First published in 1845, it is called a *palimpsest,* which is a Greek word meaning 'rescraped', because someone rubbed out the original text and wrote over the top of it. Fortunately it is possible to discover the original, which is the New Testament text. The text is similar to *Codex Vaticanus. Ephraemi* is in the National Library of Paris.

There are many more codices, but as they become progressively later in date, they are of less interest for our particular purpose. There are ongoing debates over whether these codices have been preserved because of their accuracy or simply because they were not used as they were unreliable. However, the one thing that we can affirm without argument is that by early in the fourth century complete sets of the Bible, as well as separate collections of New Testament books, were circulating among the churches.

Early translations of the Bible

With the annexation of Greece as part of the Roman Empire in the middle of the second century BC, Greek became virtually the second language of the Empire. Although the civil service operated through the medium of Latin, virtually the whole of cultural and social life used Greek. For this reason all our earliest texts, whether the writings of the church leaders or the fragments of Scripture, are in Greek. During AD 180 Irenaeus wrote his monumental treatise against the heretics in Greek, and yet he was Bishop of Lyons! Across Western Europe, therefore, there was little need for the Gospels and apostles to be translated into Latin. As late as AD 200 Hippolytus of Rome was still using Greek for his valuable Christian writing.

However, the situation was different in North Africa where Latin was the common language. Souter is confident that 'In Tertullian's time a Latin New Testament already existed in Africa';[17] that is, early in the third century. However, the reference to a 'New Testament' does not mean that we have a neat twenty-seven book edition. All that remains are parts of most of the books from the New Testament from a variety of texts. But it is sufficient to suggest that most, if not all, of the canon was circulating in Latin across North Africa at this time.

The development of translations in the West was slower for the reason given. But by the time of Jerome, as we saw in chapter 6, a full Latin translation (the *Vulgate*) of the twenty-seven books as we know them was available for all the churches well before the close of the fourth century.

A summary of the evidence from the papyri and codices

- The Chester Beatty Papyri prove that before AD 200 New Testament books circulated as small groups, especially Paul's letters, since it would be too expensive for one codex to contain all twenty-seven books.
- The John Rylands Papyrus shows that within a few decades of the death of the apostle John, his Gospel was available in Egypt as a complete book. Luke was circulating around the same time.
- Most of the New Testament books were available in North Africa early in the third century as Latin translations.
- The early codices, principally *Sinaiticus* and *Vaticanus*, demonstrate that the New Testament was circulating as a

complete document in book form early in the fourth century.

- The evidence of the Greek texts and Latin translations agree with the literature of the church leaders, that there were never any other Gospels than the four that were used and accepted by all the churches.
- It is important to remember that this evidence of the manuscripts and codices provides us with the earliest *known* and *certain* date for the circulation of the New Testament books; it is almost certain that similar collections were circulating earlier.

10. More bits and pieces
— the earliest papyrus fragments

In 1996 a storm of scholarly debate was aroused by the publication of *The Jesus Papyrus*. In this book Carsten Thiede, working in Germany as a recognized expert in the field of dating early writing, dated three fragments of papyrus held in the library at Magdalen College, Oxford. They had been indisputably identified as part of Matthew 26 and Thiede asserted that they were written some years before the fall of Jerusalem in AD 70. The book quickly became a best-seller, spawned a TV documentary and raised strong discussion with experts lining up to agree or disagree. The case may not be proved, but either way, it is yet another indication that those who insist on a late date for the writing of the Gospels would be wise to think again.

This next section is presented in some detail for those who like a little detective work! The subject is not at all central to the development of the New Testament canon, but is of interest in evidencing an early date for the individual books. We are dealing here with very small fragments of text, but they are by no means unimportant, as we shall see.

The science of papyrology is the highly skilled task of taking a small sample of ancient parchment and identifying what it is: its place of origin, its date and, even more important, what piece of literature it represents. Sometimes the papyrologist is working with a tiny fragment of a few words, some indecipherable or broken, over just a few lines. It may seem an impossible task, but it isn't for the worker skilled in languages and ancient documents.

A simple illustration will show how it is possible to identify the book from which a small fragment is taken. If you were to rip out a page from this book you are reading, then tear a one-inch diameter section at random from any part of that page, you would be left with approximately fifty letters, or parts of letters, over five lines. It would be possible to reconstruct most of the incomplete letters by your knowledge of the English language, though this would not complete all the words for you. The 'predictive text' on a modern phone and 'auto correction' on a computer illustrate how extremely accurate this can be. Surprising though it may seem, having got this far, and given such factors as size, typeface and spacing, it is virtually impossible that your small fragment would fit any other book in existence than this particular publication. It may take you some time to narrow down your search to this book, but once found, your identification could be exact. That is what the science of papyrology is about.

In what follows, we will trace the intriguing story of some of the oldest fragments of the New Testament. For our purpose, it does not matter that they are only fragments — it is their existence and their date that matters. For example, if it could be proved without any shadow of doubt that a fragment of one of the Gospels had been discovered and dated well before the end of the first century, say at around AD 68, then it would be proved without question that that Gospel, or a significant part of it, was in existence at that time — and that the original must have been written earlier. We do not need to find the complete document to come to this conclusion.

Again, to use an illustration, many books published in the nineteenth century did not carry a date of publication, and at times this is most frustrating for researchers. However, if the researcher discovers a dated letter in which the writer quotes from that particular book, or better still a fragment of one of the pages which, by the context of where it was found, can be accurately dated, then at least he can affirm that the book itself was written sometime prior to that known date. That is what papyrologists, with the aid of other specialists, aim to do.

Radiocarbon dating is of little use to the papyrologists concerned with the texts that follow, for two reasons. In the first place, that method can only be accurate to plus or minus fifty years, and that is far too wide a margin of error for our purposes. Secondly, the method demands the destruction of the material offered for sample, and whilst this is only a few grams, it would often mean the loss of vital letters or even spaces from the original. Dating is therefore mainly by the type of ink and parchment or papyrus used, the handwriting and known characteristics of style — in much the same way that a modern forensic handwriting expert would operate — and of course any artefacts that are found in the same location.

We are now ready to look at a few of the earliest known 'scraps' of the New Testament. When Sir Frederick Kenyon, then director of the British Museum, wrote in 1936 that the Chester Beatty Papyri were 'the earliest copies of the Bible as yet known to exist',[1] he little knew what lay only a few years ahead.

Qumran fragment 7Q5 — a fragment from Mark's Gospel?

Among the fragments that had been found from 1947 onwards in the caves around the Dead Sea, one lay unidentified for years in the Rockefeller Museum in Jerusalem. Whilst checking the catalogue of biblical manuscripts in the Vatican Library in Rome, Jose O'Callaghan found himself intrigued by a small text discovered in cave 7 at Qumran as late as 1955 and labelled simply as 'Fragment not identified. 7Q5'. Cave 7 was separate from the other Qumran caves and much closer to Jericho.

Among his many qualifications, Father Jose O'Callaghan was Professor of Greek Papyrology and Palaeography at the Pontifical Biblical Institute in Rome, and he has been described as 'an accomplished papyrologist whose previous publications have been characterized by scholarly insight and balanced judgement'.[2] O'Callaghan has therefore long been recognized as a leading scholar in his field and he studied the original 7Q5 document in the Rockefeller Museum.

7Q5 was part of eighteen fragments all written in Greek (not Aramaic) and on papyrus (not parchment) that were discovered scattered on the floor of the cave; it was also part of a scroll (not a codex) since the writing was on one side of the papyrus only, and it was in a clearly identifiable 'decorative' capital (uncial) script. All this was important information. The 7Q5 fragment contained only nineteen letters, half of them incomplete, on just five lines.

That may not sound much, but a papyrologist of O'Callaghan's experience was used to working with less than this. The same cave had revealed twenty-two letters on five lines that had been confidently identified as part of the apocryphal book Baruch 6:43–44. By comparison, the oldest known papyrus fragment of Virgil, discovered at Masada in 1989, contains fifteen letters (two of which are almost illegible) on one line, and these have been reliably identified as Aeneid 4:9 — and no one questions this. So, this small fragment is well within the workspace of an experienced papyrologist.

Jose O'Callaghan focused on four letters: *n n e s*, and eventually concluded that they must be part of the word

Gennesaret. That could have come from the Apocryphal book
1 Maccabees 11:67, but the rest of the text simply would not
fit that verse. This drew him to the same word found in the
New Testament Gospel of Mark. The whole fragment neatly
fitted the space required for Mark 6:52–53. There was even
a blank space, the length of almost three letters, at the end of
our verse 52, which was a known way of indicating a break
long before verse numbers had been added.

What made this discovery even more challenging was
the fact that the contents of cave 7 had already been fixed
as having been deposited no later than AD 68 and there is
no evidence that it was ever reopened until archaeologists
discovered the cave in 1955. Attempts have been made to
suggest that perhaps Christians revisited the cave after that
date and then deposited the text, but this is a forlorn hope
by the critics. Carsten Thiede, whose work on another text
(P64) we will consider below, has commented: 'All serious
archaeological investigation has discounted the idea that ...
the Qumran caves were re-inhabited after AD 68.'[3]

More than this, long before O'Callaghan had identified the
text, experts had dated the actual writing as no later than the
end of the first century.[4] In fact, the same decorative uncial
script — though in copies of pagan philosophers — has been
found in the remains of Herculaneum in Italy which was
covered in volcanic ash by Mount Vesuvius in AD 79. Thus
the conclusion is simple: these fragments from the Dead Sea
cave 7 are evidence of manuscripts of the Christian New
Testament, written in neat decorative script, before AD 68.[5]
And since these are assumed to be copies and not by the hand
of the original writers, the autographs must go back much
earlier.

O'Callaghan published his work in many journals and, as
would be expected when an early New Testament text is found,
there were many who opposed his conclusions;[6] generally, it

should be noted, the opposition came from New Testament critical scholars and theologians and not from the scientists. Someone was quick to point out the relevance of part of the text of Mark 6:52: 'they had not understood ... their hearts were hardened'!

In 1994 'one of the greatest papyrologists of our time', Orsolina Montevecchi, then Honorary President of the International Papyrologists Association, concluded: 'I do not think that there can be any doubt about the identification of 7Q5.'[7]

After years of debate, no satisfactory alternative explanation has been offered for the existence of a text from the Gospel of Mark in a cave whose contents were sealed by AD 68, and in which there is no evidence of later intrusion. Had the conclusions run the other way, they would have been accepted without question, but because all the known evidence to date points to the completion *and copying* of the Gospel of Mark, or at least part of it, well before the fall of Jerusalem in AD 70, it apparently must be resisted at all costs.

From the same cave 7Q4 — a fragment from 1 Timothy?

O'Callaghan claims that nine other fragments from the same cave fit perfectly parts of the New Testament, especially 1 Timothy 3:16, 4:1-3 (7Q4); Mark 4:28 (7Q6); and James 1:23, 24 (7Q8).[8] The suggestion that 1 Timothy and James could be found in texts dating before AD 68 is a conclusion that John Wenham sympathetically admits 'is almost too shocking to be contemplated!'[9]

Significantly, the most vigorous arguments against this identification from 1 Timothy comes from those who do not believe that Paul wrote the letter to Timothy. However, the strength of 7Q4 on these verses in Timothy is that it contains the *end* of five lines, which makes it far easier to identify — try discovering more than one piece of literature with five consecutive lines that close with identical words, all copied before AD 68! The odds against this are astronomical.

Whether or not O'Callaghan is correct in every case, the portions referred to above, and not least 7Q5 and 7Q4, are virtually certain. No other identifications have been offered for these fragments, and if it were not for the fact that they are very early evidence of portions of the Gospels and letters of Paul, there would be little debate about most of them.

The evidence is that well before the destruction of Herculaneum in AD 79, or of Jerusalem in AD 70, Christians were using copies of their sacred texts — the Gospels and the letters of Paul for example — from the best decorative scripts possible.

O'Callaghan claims to have found in this cave, fragments from Mark, Acts, Romans, 1 Timothy, 2 Peter and James — a fair sample of the New Testament canon!

A summary of the evidence from 7Q5 and 4:

- All archaeologists agree that the contents of Qumran cave 7 were deposited before AD 68 and that the cave was never revisited until 1955.
- The script of the Mark fragment has been identified as no later than the close of the first century.
- Some of the world's leading papyrologists have identified the fragment as taken from Mark 6.
- All scholars agree that the fragment is a copy, in which case the original must be earlier than AD 68.
- The fragment from 1 Timothy is hard to dispute since it contains the end of five consecutive lines.

In 1846 the German liberal critic of the Bible, D. F. Strauss, suggested that 'It would be an argument of decisive weight in favour of the credibility of the biblical history, could it indeed be shown that it was written by eye-witnesses or even by persons nearly contemporaneous with the events narrated.'[10] Here, then, is the first part of that evidence. After the publication of O'Callaghan's work, *Time* magazine commented that it was now time 'to make a bonfire of seventy tons of indigestible German scholarship'.

The Magdalen Fragment P64 — a fragment from Matthew's Gospel?

This story concerns three small scraps of parchment belonging to Magdalen College in Oxford. The largest, identified by Carsten Thiede, Director of the Institute for Basic Epistemological Research in Paderborn, Germany, contained fragments of Matthew 26. The text that Thiede was working on had been discovered in Upper Egypt by the Rev. Charles Bousfield Huleatt in 1901. Shortly before the tragic death of Huleatt and his family in an earthquake at Messinesi on 28 December 1908, he sent these fragments of an ancient text to his alma mater at Magdalen College, where they were duly filed as 'P. Magdalen Greek 17/P64' and remained unidentified for almost half a century.[11]

The papyrologist Colin H. Roberts worked on these texts in the 1950s and published his work 'An Early Papyrus of the First Gospel' in 1953 in the *Harvard Theological Review*.[12] He noted that the largest was only 4.1 cm by 1.3 cm. On this fragment there would have been 15 or 16 letters to a line and it was written in double column to a page, and was probably bound into a book on its own that would have amounted to some 150 pages. The fragments, written on both sides of the page, contain parts of Matthew 28:7–8, 10, 14–15, 22–23, 31–33. The largest section contained thirty-seven letters (or parts of letters) over four lines. Roberts dated the fragments as late in the second century, which made them at least the oldest known texts of Matthew's Gospel.

Carsten Thiede undertook detailed and careful research on the fragments and came to a very different conclusion from Roberts. The fact that P64 is part of a codex rather than a scroll does not at all preclude a much earlier date for it. The Italian papyrologist, Italo Gallo, has shown that the codex was in common use by Christians 'not later than 70 AD'.[13] This is now generally accepted. Similarly, the form of writing in the Magdalen fragment — Greek capitals, or *uncial* as they are known — is virtually identical to the writing of a fragment also discovered in Egypt, though not a biblical text, that dates itself as the twelfth year of the Emperor Nero, which is AD 66.[14] Similarly, the presence of shorthand forms for the divine names in the text (*nomina sacra*) is known to have been used before the turn of the first century. And the handwriting used in the Magdalen fragments is very similar to other texts dated in the first century.

Thiede dated these fragments to sometime before AD 70, and commented on the early date of this fragment of Matthew's Gospel:

> This is an unpalatable conclusion for New Testament scholars convinced that St Matthews's Gospel is a later, community creation, describing Jesus ... in a way which would meet the liturgical needs of the eighties of the first century. To some academics and many ordinary Christians however, already convinced that the Gospels consist of authentic eyewitness material from apostolic times, the result had come as no surprise.[15]

This perceptive comment perhaps shows why many theologians and New Testament scholars have been so reluctant to accept the results of Thiede's careful work — presuppositions are hard to abandon.

If Thiede is correct, it means that the full text from which P64 is a small part could have been copied in the lifetime of Matthew himself. Thiede comments that 'The instinct to undermine the Gospels has overtaken the pre-modern instinct to take their truth for granted... Some scholars and writers will go to almost any length to avoid the charge of credulity.'[16]

We may recall the comments of John Robinson in chapter 1 who referred to 'the consistent evasion by modern commentators of a solution they have already prejudged to be impossible'.[17]

The Barcelona Papyri P67 — more from Matthew's Gospel

This document is housed at the Fundación San Lucas Evangelista, in Barcelona.[18] The Barcelona Papyri consist of two fragments containing parts of Matthew 3:9, 15 and 5:20–22, 25–28 and are clearly part of a codex because they are written on both sides.

The papyrologist Colin Roberts accepted that both P67 and P64 were most likely written by the same hand (though probably not part of the same codex) and this has since been confirmed independently by Carsten Thiede and Philip Comfort.[19] Because of their uncial style Roberts dated them to the second century. However, this careful scribal style predates the first century and this means that the once generally accepted date of early second century might now be revised to well before the close of the first century.

The Paris Papyrus P4 — something from Luke's Gospel

This papyrus, held at the Bibliothèque Nationale in Paris, is larger than both the Magdalen (P64) and Barcelona (P67) fragments and contains large parts of Luke 1 – 6. It is not linked with the other two, though may have come from the same scribal school and only a little later in date. Thiede dates it as around AD 70 whilst Comfort is more cautious at early in the second century.[20] What is virtually certain, therefore, is that we have a significant portion of Luke's Gospel circulating in neat uncial format early in the second century at the latest.

Around the corner?

There are many more odds and ends that could be described: P77 is a small papyrus fragment from a codex of Matthew 23:30–39, originally dated late second century, then AD 150, but it could be much older. P1 resides in the university of Pennsylvania and is a good example of Matthew 1:1–9, 12, 14–20, which may be not much older than the Magdalen fragments.

However, much more may yet come to light. There are many unopened and as yet uncovered scrolls at Herculaneum, the city devastated by Vesuvius in AD 79. We know there was a Christian community here, so what texts may they have been using? Whilst the arguments in favour of an early date for any one of these fragments may be disputed — and certainly will be by critics because too much swings on the evidence — the cumulative data is a powerful argument for the circulation of copies of the New Testament records well before the close of the first century.

Summary of the evidence of these fragments

- The papyrus fragment 7Q5 comes from a Dead Sea cave sealed in AD 68 and unopened until 1955. It is part of a scroll of

Mark's Gospel. Fragments from Timothy, Mark and James may also be identified in the same cave.

- Other codex fragments containing parts of Matthew's Gospel and Luke's Gospel could be dated as early as AD 70.
- The evidence is that well before the destruction of Jerusalem in AD 70, Christians were using copies of their sacred texts — the Gospels and the letters of Paul for example — from the best decorative scripts possible.

11. An epilogue

This final chapter will add nothing new to the debate so far, but will attempt to survey the evidence and assess the conclusions. The subject of the canon of the New Testament is detailed and complicated and any attempt to oversimplify can lead to inaccuracies that border on untruth. To make the subject accessible, it has been necessary to ignore some areas of detail, but nothing has been overlooked in order to avoid embarrassment. The facts have been faced as fairly as possible.

The whole issue of the canon has come to the fore with the publication of scurrilous novels and scandalous 'academic' attacks. Often both have penetrated the subject as profoundly as a pond skater penetrates the water. However, those who believe the Bible to have a divine origin and who value it for their daily lives are often ill equipped to handle a reply to the casual defamation of the New Testament canon.

The wild claim that 'More than eighty gospels were considered for the New Testament', and the only slightly less absurd assertion that 'The four Gospels that made it into the official canon, were chosen, more or less arbitrarily, out of a large sample of at least a dozen'[1] have been shown to be as banal as they first appeared. There were never any other Gospels that jockeyed for a place in the canon — not one. Of all the books over which questions did arise in one corner of the empire or another, the four Gospels were not among them. In fact, if the whole of the history of the development of the canon was as straightforward as that of Matthew, Mark, Luke and John, there would hardly be a need for any book on the subject.

When Paul wrote to the church at Thessalonica he commended their discernment which meant that, 'When you received the word of God, which you heard from us, you accepted it not as the word of men, but as it actually is, the word of God, which is at work in you who believe' (1 Thessalonians 2:13). In other words, they recognized the intrinsic authority of Paul's preaching, and presumably recognized his writing in the same way.

A chief conclusion has been that the canon of the New Testament is based upon the essential authority of the books themselves. No church or council of bishops created a canon or invested the books with authority, churches simply recognized the authority of each book that existed from the moment it was written.

However, this does not preclude a rational debate about the human factors that controlled the development of the canon. Understanding the interplay between divine providence, self-authentication and human judgement is essential in the discussion over the canon, as in many areas of Christian theology.

It is sometimes suggested that the large amount of written material, including the false gospels and letters, that was spawned in the first hundred years after the death of the apostles, undermines the claim that we have the correct books in our canon. On the contrary, that very surplus demonstrates how incredible it is that whilst not all the twenty-seven were accepted universally and at once, not one other 'non-canonical' book ever became a serious and widespread contender for inclusion. The debate was rarely about what should be left out — that was fairly straightforward — the debate centred around what should be included.

One intriguing fact about the story of the churches in the first four centuries is that there is not one record of a squabble over the question of the canon. If we leave aside the maverick position held by the Gnostics and other sects who selected only what they wanted, we are left with the vast majority of orthodox leaders who, whilst not always recognizing precisely the same cluster of books, were always using a large mix of the twenty-seven.

There are only rare examples of non-canonical books intruding into the library of authoritative Scriptures: the Epistle of Barnabas and the Shepherd of Hermas occasionally may have been considered — but the Gospel of Thomas, never.

In chapter 1 the claim was made that long before there was a directory of twenty-seven books, there were twenty-seven books being used as Scripture. Thus the authority lies in the books themselves rather than in the canon. William Barclay expressed this well when he claimed: 'It is the simple truth to say that the New Testament books became canonical because no one could stop them doing so.'[2]

Bruce Metzger provides an excellent summary of this position when he suggests:

> If the authority of the New Testament books resides not in the circumstances of their conclusion with a collection made by the Church, but in the source from which they came, then the New Testament was in principle complete when the various elements coming from this source had been written.[3]

Comparing the rubbish

The average 'man in the street' who contemptuously dismisses the New Testament as an accident of history has almost certainly never read either the New Testament or the documents that might have contended for inclusion. To read the Gospel of Luke and then to settle down with the Gospel of the Egyptians would be quite sufficient to illustrate what is meant by the 'intrinsic' authority of the canonical books. As William Barclay has well commented on the books that never entered the canon: 'To read them and then to read the New Testament is to enter into a different world.'[4] These possible contenders for a place in the canon fall into two categories:

• Those that were well written and contained useful instruction for the churches, but whose writers never pretended to write with apostolic authority, and indeed humbly contrasted themselves to the apostles. Polycarp, Ignatius, Justin, Irenaeus, Tertullian are typical of a host of valuable pastors in the first two centuries of the Christian church.
• Those documents that claimed to be from the hand of an apostle but clearly were not. This is the pseudepigrapha that the church leaders were not slow in identifying. Irenaeus and Tertullian, for example, entertained no doubts about the rubbish that was to be opposed, and they identified by name many of the documents that modern publishers are so eager for us to read. The Muratorian Canon reflected the view of all the orthodox leaders of the second century when it recorded: 'it is not suitable for gall to be mingled with honey.'

Whenever a new find comes into the hand of the scholars and media — a fragment here or a battered collection there

— the public is regaled with the promise of 'new light on the Bible' which will compel us to 'rethink our understanding of the traditional text', may provide 'a supplement to the Bible' and even 'create a crisis of faith'. In the event these new discoveries do nothing of the kind. All they do is reveal the very reason why such texts were discarded by the wise leaders of the church eighteen hundred years ago. It is only a foolish and gullible generation that clamours to reinstate them.

What made a book, Bible?

The Bible speaks, and countless millions of Christians over two millennia have been convinced of its authority — yet its true authority rests elsewhere than the subjective recognition of individuals.

At first the churches had no need to define what made a book special and equal to the Old Testament Scriptures. If the letter came from Paul or Peter, that was sufficient. However, it was not long before others began writing additional letters and gospels either to fill the gaps or to propagate their own ideas. Some tests became necessary and over the course of the next two hundred years five tests were used at one time or another. Each of these we have seen as the story of the canon developed.

Apostolic — does it come from an apostle?

The first Christians looked for apostolic authority for the authentic books, just as the Jews had expected theirs to be underwritten by the prophets. If the authorship of the books was unimportant, why was Paul, for example, so insistent that his readers should be reassured that the letters they received actually came from his pen (1 Corinthians 16:21; Galatians 6:11; Colossians 4:18; 2 Thessalonians 3:17; Philemon 19)? And why were others, especially the heretics, equally interested in putting out their own writings under an apostolic name (2 Thessalonians 2:2)?

Not only were the New Testament writers confident of their own divine authority (1 Thessalonians 2:13) but they accorded the same to each other also — thus Peter equates Paul's letters with 'the other Scriptures' (2 Peter 3:16). They made no hard distinction between the spoken and written word; if apostolic, they were equally authoritative (1 Thessalonians 4:2; 2 Thessalonians 2:15). This was also the test for fellowship: obedience to apostolic authority (2 Thessalonians 3:14).

In the year AD 180 Irenaeus, Bishop of Lyons, posed the question: 'How should it be if the apostles themselves had not left us writings?'[5] and he gave three tests of accepted scriptures. The first was that they should be written either by an apostle or by men closely associated with an apostle. Church leaders were at pains to declare the apostolic credentials of the Gospels. Papias was eager to establish Paul behind Luke's Gospel and Peter behind Mark's; similarly Origen might doubt that Paul was the author of Hebrews, but that Luke, his travelling companion, probably was. The Muratorian Canon rejected the Shepherd of Hermas because it was 'after the time' of the apostles.

In the second century, Tertullian records a deacon in an Asian church being severely disciplined for writing the pseudo Acts of Paul under the apostle's name; but if it was the impact of the words alone that was important, why would it matter who wrote it? Without doubt, apostolic authority was vital for the formation of the canon in the mind of the early church — even if it didn't matter to critics eighteen hundred years later.

The written word of the apostle was not merely a means by which people would be led into the truth, it *was* the truth; it was the basis of faith and the authority for it. The words of the apostles in their letters do not *become* the word of God (which is what the twentieth-century Swiss theologians Karl Barth and Emil Brunner would have us believe), they *are* the words of God — irrespective of what anyone may think about them.

Ancient — has it been used from the earliest times?

If a book was clearly apostolic by its authorship, then naturally it must have been available from the earliest days of the Christian church. When the compiler of the Muratorian Canon expressed his interest in the Shepherd of Hermas, he also recognized that it could not be numbered among the accepted books because it was too late in its composition. As stated before, the Acts of Paul was one of the earliest pieces of non-canonical writing and is not especially unhelpful in its content, but because it was compiled some time around the mid second century and its author was known to be a deacon in Asia, it was never considered among the canonical books.

Early in the fourth century, Athanasius listed the New Testament canon as we know it today and claimed that these were the books 'received by us through tradition as belonging to the Canon'.[6] At the end of that century, the council meeting at Carthage in AD 397 listed the twenty-seven books of the canon, adding that they are 'what we have received from our fathers'.

Accurate — does it conform to the accepted teaching of the churches?

There was widespread agreement among the churches across the empire as to the content of the Christian message. Irenaeus asked the question whether a particular writing was consistent with what the churches taught. This is what ruled out so much of the Gnostic material immediately.

Even though the second letter of Peter was the last book to be accepted into the universal canon, its final reception was partly the result of an acknowledgement that everything about it was consistent with apostolic authorship.

Most of the false writings betrayed themselves sooner or later at this point. Serapion, the leader at Antioch from AD 200–210, was attracted to the Gospel of Peter until, on closer inspection, he realized that it contained hints of heresy. Of all the apostles, Peter seems to have had most added to his name, possibly because in reality he has left us so little in contrast to Paul. However, the Gospel of Peter, the Acts of Peter and the Apocalypse of Peter were excluded from all canons for the simple reason that they did not contain apostolic theology.

The advent of liberal critics over the last one hundred and fifty years means that for them the canon can be as wide open as you wish, since accurate theology has little meaning. This was certainly not so for the apostles and their successors. The faith 'once and for all delivered to the saints' was vital for the health of the churches, and for this an authoritative body of books that contained the truth and nothing but the truth became more and more vital as the years passed. Without a sure canon there could be no certain theology.

Accepted — are most of the churches using it?

Naturally it took time for letters to circulate among the churches and some, like the Gospels, would probably travel more rapidly than others. After all, some of the letters of Paul dealt with local issues that another church may not immediately have seen as relevant to their situation. The difference between the books immediately accepted by the churches in the east and those in the west is interesting, but what is more significant is the fact that more rapidly than we might imagine would have been possible, the great majority of the New Testament books, some twenty-three of the twenty-seven, were almost universally accepted well before the middle of the second century, as the Muratorian Canon witnesses.

When Justin Martyr informed the emperor of the typical Christian Sunday worship meeting, he added in such a casual way that they read the 'memoirs of the apostles or the writings of the prophets' that it was assumed to be understood as a collected body of books.

Both Origen and Eusebius claimed to present a list of the books accepted 'throughout the churches'. The four Gospels, for example, were for Origen 'the only indisputable ones in the church of God under heaven'. For his part, Eusebius began his lists with the twenty-two books that were universally accepted by the churches. This was also the position of both Jerome and Augustine.

When tradition carries the weight of the overwhelming majority of churches throughout the widely scattered Christian communities across the vast Roman Empire, with no one church controlling the beliefs of all the others, it has to be taken seriously.

Authentic — does it have the ring of truth?

It is the internal witness of the texts themselves that are the strongest evidence of canonicity. The authoritative voice of the prophets, 'This is what the Lord says', is matched by the apostles claiming to write, not the words of men, but the words of God (1 Thessalonians 2:13). Does the book have that 'ring of truth' that sets it apart from other literature?

Early on, the church leaders recognized the voice of the Spirit in the books that formed the accepted canon. Origen wrote of the Scriptures breathing 'the Spirit of fullness' and added that there is nothing 'whether in the Law or in the Prophets, in the Evangelists [the Gospels] or in the Apostles, which does not descend from the fullness of the Divine Majesty'. Clement of Rome believed that Paul wrote 'under the inspiration of the Spirit'. Even when these leaders themselves wrote to the churches and believed they were led by the Spirit, they were careful always to distance themselves from the unique authority of the apostles in the Scriptures.

This was a natural progression for those who accepted the concept of inspiration that is taught in the New Testament itself. The unity of the New Testament books was, and always has been, a remarkable phenomena which is only denied by those who merely scan the surface looking for problems that, unknown to them, have been satisfactorily answered often centuries before. Certainly the leaders of the churches in the first three centuries recognized the books that 'belonged' together and those that, even though they may be useful, were of an altogether different family.

Not one of these five tests may be sufficient in itself. Even if the first is considered indispensable then some may find difficulty presenting a hard and fast case for Luke or Mark or Hebrews. However, it was the cumulative evidence of all five, not least the first, that led to the steady, growing, strength of the books that all eventually settled into the recognized canon — without rivals.

A canon in mind

The first formal statement of a canon of New Testament books by a council of bishops was at Carthage in AD 397. It is likely that the synod at Hippo four years earlier made a similar recommendation, but there are no records of that meeting available today. Since that date, no one has seriously suggested adding any book to the canon, though a few mavericks (and even Luther must be included here) suggested taking some out.[7]

However, it would take a strange blindness to the evidence to suggest that there was no canon before this date. At Carthage, all the New Testament books were placed in our present order, but the Muratorian Canon had presented the same with only four missing as early as AD 150, Origen had established his own list (the same as our twenty-seven) in AD 240, Eusebius in AD 325 and Athanasius in 367. Each of these only reflected what the great majority of the churches believed. Wenham is conservative to conclude that as far as churches in the West are concerned, the canon 'stretches back to the end of the fourth century with scarcely a break'.[8] We can take it back to Origen at least. In fact, the *concept* of a New Testament canon is seen well before the close of the first century by the way the Gospels and epistles are being used in the writings of the church leaders.

The evidence from the single surviving letter of Polycarp is highly significant. In that one letter to the church at Philippi he quoted from sixteen New Testament books, and no others, and appears to assume that his readers would be familiar with his source — and this soon after AD 110! It is virtually impossible not to appreciate that Polycarp had a concept of a canon of authoritative apostolic books.

Similarly Clement of Rome, writing even earlier before the close of the first century, quoted freely from at least eleven New Testament books and attributed to them the same authority as that of the Hebrew Scriptures which he used. Justin Martyr confirms that by the middle of the second century the churches were using 'the memoirs of the apostles' in their services; he is referring to the four Gospels particularly.

Throughout the first three hundred years of the church, all the church leaders were using the New Testament books — and with very rare exceptions, those alone — as the authority for their teaching. A canon may not have been compiled, but it was certainly assumed.

The books of the New Testament (as with the Old as well) did not come as most world religions allegedly received their holy books. The Koran was supposedly revealed by the angel Gabriel to one man in Mecca and Medina; the Book of Mormon came on golden plates revealed to one man. By contrast the New Testament is the work of eight or nine writers over a period of thirty or so years and yet without any contradiction in their message. The canon came to us, as one writer expresses it, 'in a quiet, shuffling sort of way'.[9]

Unlike, for example, the Koran, where there is rarely an open debate on the wide differences between the various texts, or an honest investigation into the dark sides of its author's life, the canon of the New Testament is open for debate and has been all along. The most vigorous critics have taken full advantage of this liberty and still the canon stands unscathed.

Back to providence

The claim was made in chapter 3 that, 'Our final appeal is not to man, not even to the early church leaders, but to God, who by his Holy Spirit has put his seal upon the New Testament. By their spiritual content and by the claim of their human writers, the twenty-seven books of our New Testament form part of the "God-breathed" Scripture.' Of course, not all would allow divine intervention and they assess the canon purely as a development of human agencies.[10]

However, providence is vital to the whole concept of revelation from beginning to end. When God revealed his word in the Scriptures, he did so by the Holy Spirit superintending men, and when he revealed himself incarnate, he did so through his Son in human form. So it is hardly a novelty to discern the hand of providence in the steady development of the canon.

The often convoluted way in which a particular book was accepted in one place but not another is perfectly in line with the way the Scriptures were 'inspired by God' in the first place. God used men to write down his word, and thus we can recognize the human characteristics of various writers. However, the divine intervention ensured that the whole body of Scripture is without error.

In the same way, it is perfectly correct to allow this divine intervention to guard the process by which eventually all the canonical books — and no others — were universally accepted. The idea of the final canon being an accident, and that any number of books could have ended up in the Bible, ignores the evident unity and provable accuracy of the whole collection of twenty-seven books.

Once again, Metzger says it well: 'There are, in fact, no historical data that prevent one from acquiescing in the conviction held by the Church Universal that, despite the very human factors ... in the production, preservation, and collection of the books of the New Testament, the whole process can also be rightly characterized as the result of divine overruling.'[11]

A belief in the authority and inerrancy of Scripture is inevitably and inextricably bound to a belief in the divine preservation of the canon. It would be as illogical to believe in a Scripture that was divinely superintended in its transmission through men but lost in the collection of books, as it would be to believe in a canon that was divinely superintended yet contained Scriptures that are full of human error. Each stands or falls with the other.

Summary of the book

The following summary should only be read in the light of the full text.

- Divine providence cannot be excluded in our discussion of the canon of the New Testament (chapter 1).
- The evidence of the New Testament critical scholar, J. A. T. Robinson, concluded that all the New Testament books were complete before AD 70 and he warned against the 'entrenched prejudice', 'tenuous deductions' and the 'tyranny of unexamined assumptions' of much modern scholarship (chapter 1).
- The canon of the Old Testament was settled by the Jews long before the time of Christ and the apostles. The Apocrypha never formed part of this canon (chapter 2).
- From the earliest records of the church leaders they frequently referred to and quoted from the Gospels and epistles as authoritative Scripture (chapter 3).
- Long before we have an authoritative canon of twenty-seven books, we have twenty-seven books being used as authoritative (chapter 3).
- By the middle of the second century the 'memoirs of the apostles' were being used regularly in Christian worship (chapter 3).
- Given the conditions of the time, a list of recognized books was not slow in forming, but remarkably rapid (chapter 3).
- In the period immediately after the death of the apostles, the churches were blessed with many leaders of high intellect who were well read in the classical literature of the day, and who never wrote under a pseudonym and never claimed apostolic authority (chapters 4 and 5).
- No one could read both the writings of the heretics and the letters of the church leaders without recognizing that they come from an entirely different family (chapters 7 and 8).

An epilogue

- By AD 180 all but seven of the New Testament books had been universally accepted by the churches. All were being used regularly with the exception of 2 Peter (chapter 5).
- The Muratorian Canon, dated around AD 150, contains all but four of our New Testament canon (chapter 5).
- All the evidence is that the churches from the earliest times were gathering the books of the New Testament, but there is no evidence that other writings were so eagerly accepted (chapter 5).
- From 180 onwards the four Gospels, Acts and thirteen letters of Paul were accepted without question across the empire. No other gospels were ever considered (chapter 6).
- By the middle of the fourth century the canon of Athanasius was identical to ours (chapter 6).
- Not until the Council at Carthage in AD 397 do we have an officially sanctioned list. Yet that list had been assumed by the majority of churches for more than one hundred years (chapter 11).
- Compared with other contemporary literature, the copies of New Testament documents are closer to the originals in time by many centuries (chapter 9).
- *Codex Sinaiticus* and *Vaticanus* confirm that the complete New Testament was circulating early in the fourth century (chapter 9).
- Papyrus fragments evidence that some New Testament books were circulating as far away as Egypt before AD 68 (chapter 10).
- Returning to providence: just as we believe in a divinely inspired transmission of the text of Scripture so we are entitled to believe in a divinely guarded transmission of the canon of Scripture — and the evidence demonstrates this. Without a sure canon there can be no certain theology.

Appendix 1
Church Fathers, unknown authors and heretics

Note that this is not intended as a complete list but those church leaders, unknown writers and heretics who are referred to in this book. The dates in most cases are approximate and may differ by a few years in various authorities.

Name	City of leadership	Dates (m = martyred)	Chief work	Contribution to the idea of a canon
Clement	Rome (Italy)	c. 95	Letter to the Corinthians	Quoted from or referred to more than half NT books and believed Paul wrote 'in the Spirit' and were 'Scriptures'.
Ignatius	Antioch (Syria)	50 – 115m	Seven letters on his way to martyrdom	Widely alluded to most of NT and used only these for his authority. They were 'the ordinances of the Lord and of the Apostles'.
Polycarp	Smyrna (Asia)	70 – 155m	Letter to the Philippians	Quoted from 16 NT books, and no others, to challenge the church. Referred to them as 'Sacred Scriptures'.

Why 27?

Name	City of leadership	Dates (m = martyred)	Chief work	Contribution to the idea of a canon
Papias	Hierapolis (Phrygia)	69 – 135m	Testimony to the authorship of Mark and Matthew.	Clearly familiar with John's Gospel, 1 Peter, 1 John and Revelation. Also had access to oral teachings.
The *Didache*		c. 50 – 80	Author unknown. Practical Christian teaching.	The author knew and quoted from Matthew but of little value in determining what was accepted.
Epistle of Barnabas		c. 130	Author unknown. Against Judaeisers in the church.	He quotes from the NT but is of little value in determining what was accepted.
The Shepherd of Hermas	Rome	c. 150	The author Hermas is unknown. Visions, commandments and parables.	Of little value in determining what was accepted.
The Muratorian Canon	Rome?	150 – 200	Author unknown. The oldest known list of NT books.	The complete NT with the exception of 1 and 2 Peter, James and Hebrews.
Justin	Rome	100 –165m	Two *Apologia* addressed to the emperor Titus, and a Dialogue with Trypho the Jew.	Defended the apostolic authority of the Four Gospels. Introduced quotations by 'it is written'. Used Revelation and familiar with Paul's letters.
Dionysius	Corinth (Greece)	c. 165	Many pastoral letters to the churches. Only small fragments remain of his letter to Rome.	He contrasts his own letters with 'the Scriptures (writings) of the Lord.'

216

Appendix 1

Name	City of leadership	Dates (m = martyred)	Chief work	Contribution to the idea of a canon
Tatian	Rome	110 – 180	Harmony of the Four Gospels (Diatessaron). An Address to the Greeks.	Only the Four Gospels accepted by the churches.
Aristides	Athens (Greece)	Writing c. 126	An Apology to Emperor Hadrian	No reference from Scripture but to the Gospel and Christian 'books'. Assumed Hadrian could access these.
Athenagoras	Athens	c. 133 – 190	A Plea for the Christians to Emperor Marcus Aurelius (AD 170). And On the Resurrection of the Dead	A few quotations from the Gospels and the epistles, but more would not be appropriate since his work is addressed to the emperor.
Irenaeus	Lugdunum (Lyons)	130 – 202	Against Heresies and defended the four Gospels.	Quoted over 1000 passages from all but four or five NT books. They are 'Holy Scriptures' given by the Holy Spirit. Revelation was a favourite book.
The Scilitan Martyrs	Carthage (N. Africa)	180m	On trial before proconsul Saturninus.	The epistles of Paul circulating in Latin in North Africa by AD 180. Almost certainly also the Four Gospels.
Tertullian	Carthage	155 – 220	Apologeticus: defence of the Christian faith. Spectaculis: theology and against heretics.	The first serious expositor and used almost all the NT books. They were equated with OT and he referred to 'the majesty of our Scriptures.' He clearly possessed a canon almost, if not wholly, identical to ours. He referred to the 'New Testament'.

Why 27?

Name	City of leadership	Dates (m = martyred)	Chief work	Contribution to the idea of a canon
Cyprian	Carthage	210 –258m	*The Unity of the Church* and many letters.	Quoted from almost ten per cent of NT and as 'Scripture'.
Hippolytus	Rome	170 – 235m	Forty works including commentaries and Christian doctrine. And *A Refutation of all Heresies.*	Used much of the NT and as 'Scripture'. Quoted from other books but not with the same authority.
Clement	Alexandria (Egypt)	153 – 216	*Exhortation to the Heathen.* *The Instructor.* *The Miscellanies.*	Quoted from all but five NT books more than 3,000 times and believed them to be 'Scripture'. No other books given the same authority. He referred to the 'New Testament'.
Origen	Alexandria	180 – 253	Great biblical scholar. Expounded almost all books of the Bible. Referred to the 'New Testament'.	By AD 240 he listed the 27 books of our canon as 'Scripture'.
Eusebius	Caesarea (Judea)	260 – 340	*Ecclesiastical History* – the 'Father of Church History'.	Listed 22 books as unquestioned by any church. The other five (James, Jude, 2 Peter and 2 and 3 John) were widely used among the churches.

Appendix 1

Name	City of leadership	Dates (m = martyred)	Chief work	Contribution to the idea of a canon
Athanasius	Alexandria	296 – 373	A strong defender of the truth against Arius who denied the deity of Christ. He also distinguished between heretical books and useful (though not canonical) books.	Next to the Muratorian Canon, Athanasius provides the oldest list of NT books (identical with our 27): 'Let no one add to them, nor take anything from them' (AD 367). He was the first to use the word 'canon' for the 27.
Augustine	Hippo (N. Africa)	354 – 430	Confessions; Letters and The City of God.	Adopted the canon of Athanasius.
Jerome	Rome & Antioch etc.	347 – 420	Commentaries and the complete Bible in Latin: the Vulgate.	Adopted the canon of Athanasius.

Some heretics

Name	Place of influence	Dates	Chief work	Chief heresy
Marcion	Rome and elsewhere	85 – 160	Only one book Antisthenes (Contradictions). But one of the earliest exponents of Gnostic views.	Gnosticism. Rejection of entire Old Testament and selection of a few New Testament books.

Why 27?

Name	Place of influence	Dates	Chief work	Chief heresy
Montanus	Asia	c. 150	Joined by Prisca and Maximilla; his 'prophe-cies' and 'revelations' were equal to Scripture.	Montanism, a form of extreme Pentecostalism.
Valentinus	Alexandria and Rome	100 – 160	Opened an in-fluential school in Rome. Pos-sibly the author of the Gospel of Truth.	Gnosticism.
Praxeas	Rome	c. 190		Monarchianism — a denial of the Trinity.
Marcus	Disciple of Valentinus	c. 175	Leader of the Morcosians.	Gnosticism.
Basilides	Alexandria	117 – 138	Twenty-four books of Exegetica. Only fragments remain.	Gnosticism.
Carpocrates	Alexandria	c. 150	Founded a Gnostic sect. Opposed by Irenaeus.	Practised magic and spiritism.

Appendix 2
A selection of collected canons

This appendix provides a summary of the earliest evidence of complete canons. Not all are covered earlier in this book.

The Muratorian Canon — c. 150
This is the earliest list available to date and is substantially the same as the final canon. It includes the four Gospels, Acts, thirteen letters of Paul, Jude, two (perhaps all three) letters of John and the Revelation of John. These are accepted by the 'universal church'. This leaves out: 1 and 2 Peter, James and Hebrews. However, 1 Peter was widely accepted by this time and may be an oversight by the writer (or the later copyist).

Origen of Alexandria — c. 240
Origen listed all twenty-seven books though recognized that not all accepted 2 and 3 John and 2 Peter. He did not know who wrote Hebrews, but accepted it as canonical: 'The thoughts are those of the apostle [Paul].'

Eusebius of Caesarea — c. 313
Eusebius listed the accepted books, disputed books and the rejected books. Those universally accepted were the twenty-

seven (and no others) with the exception of five listed as disputed by some: James, Jude, 2 Peter and 2 and 3 John. Eusebius admits they were known to most of the churches and he himself accepted them.

Cyril of Jerusalem — c. 350
Twenty-six books are listed (only the Apocalypse of John is missing). Hebrews is accepted as Paul's. 'Let all the rest be put aside in a secondary rank'; and Cyril warns that they are not even worth reading privately.

The Cheltenham Canon — c. 360
Identified in 1885 (and sometimes referred to as the Mommsen list after its discoverer) it is thought to reflect the position in North Africa. Only James, Jude and Hebrews are not mentioned by name, but there is room for at least two of these in the list. No non-canonical books are included.

The Council of Laodicea — c. 363
Identical to that of Athanasius except that the Apocalypse of John is missing. It commands that only these should be read in the churches, though Westcott and others question whether the list is a later addition and not the conclusions of the Council itself.

Athanasius of Alexandria — c. 367
In his *Festal Epistle* for the year 367 he listed the entire canon exactly as we have it today in content though Esther is missing from the Old Testament, and the order varies: Paul's epistles follow those of Peter, John, Jude and James, and Hebrews comes before 1 Timothy — a strong indication that Athanasius believed Hebrews belonged to Paul. Athanasius concludes: 'These are the fountains of salvation, that he who thirsts may

Appendix 2

be satisfied with the living words they contain. In these alone the teaching of godliness is proclaimed. Let no one add to these; let nothing be taken away from them.'

Tyrannius Rufinus — c. 380
Well reflects the churches in the west. His canon was the same as that of Athanasius (except that the order differed) and he listed additional books that were useful but not canonical, and those 'that should not be read out in church'.

Jerome — c. 380
The monk who dedicated himself to producing the Latin Vulgate, which is still the official version for the Roman Catholic Church, adopted the same canon as did Augustine who was only ten years younger than Jerome.

Augustine — c. 390
Augustine was present at the Synods of Hippo (AD 393) and Carthage (397 and again in 419) at which the canon of twenty-seven books was recognized as the one in use universally among the western churches. No known records of Hippo exist and Carthage may reflect what was stated there.

Gregory of Nazianzus — c. 350
Produced in metrical form, presumably for easy remembrance, it includes all with the exception of the Apocalypse of John. Gregory concludes: 'If there is anything outside of these it is not among the genuine books.'[1]

The apostolic canons — c. 380
The origin and authorship is uncertain. Twenty-seven books are listed, but this includes two of Clement, which were never widely accepted.

Amphilochius of Iconium — *c.* 390
Another metrical list which includes all the twenty-seven though acknowledges that some question Hebrews, 2 Peter, 2 and 3 John, and Jude. Of Revelation 'Some approve, but the most say it is spurious.' However, nothing is included that should not be there.

The third Council of Carthage — 397
Probably the same as the first Council at Hippo in North Africa (393), though there are no records of this. Augustine was present here and again in 419 when the same list was confirmed.

The twenty-seven books were sent to the Bishop of Rome for confirmation. From here the canon was accepted universally.

The Peshitta version — *c.*390
At the end of the fourth century from Syria, only twenty-two books are listed, with 2 Peter, 2 and 3 John, Jude and Revelation missing.

Trent and Westminster
The Roman Catholic Council of Trent (1546), the Thirty-nine Articles of the Church of England (1552) and the Westminster Confession (1646) of the English and Scottish Puritan churches each stated the New Testament canon exactly as we know it today. They did not fix it or decide it, they simply declared what the church almost universally had long assumed.

John Wenham has slightly skewed the evidence when he claimed: 'There has never been complete unanimity amongst Christians as to the limits of the Canon... It was not till the Council of Hippo in 393 that something like unanimity was reached as to the limits of the New Testament Canon.'[2] It is true that *unanimity* took a while to arrive, but long before Hippo and Carthage the twenty-seven books were the only ones used across the great majority of churches as their authoritative canon.

The fact that not all agreed totally — 2 Peter was put back in by all and Revelation was left out by some — makes the point that no one church or leader was dictating to the others. Thus the near total agreement was all the more remarkable.

Appendix 3
A select bibliography

To read the early church leaders on line the best site to visit is the Christian Classics Ethereal Library: http://www.ccel.org

Carson and Woodbridge ed. *Hermeneutics, Authority and Canon,* Inter Varsity Press, Leicester, 1986. Chapter 9 by David G. Dunbar. A helpful contribution in that it briefly interacts with modern theories of the development of the canon, both liberal and conservative.

Bruce F. F. *The Books and the Parchments,* Pickering & Inglis, London, 1950. An excellent introduction, though updated by his later work.

Bruce F. F. *The Canon of Scripture,* InterVarsity Press, Illinois, 1988. Possibly the most accessible as well as scholarly book available on this subject. With this and Metzger, the serious student would need little else. It includes some useful closing essays on modern theories of the canon.

Henry, Carl F. H. *God, Revelation and Authority,* Paternoster Publishing, Carlisle, 1999. First pub. 1979. Vol. IV, chapter 18,

'The Debate over the Canon'. A clear and concise overview of the canon debate with many excellent insights.

Metzger, Bruce. *The Canon of the New Testament*, Oxford University Press, New York, Oxford, 1987. Easily the best and most thorough treatment of the subject from a contemporary scholar.
Metzger, Bruce. *The Text of the New Testament*, Oxford University Press, New York, Oxford, 1992. A full and scholarly presentation of the transmission of the New Testament text. Not the subject of the canon.

Warfield, Benjamin B. *The Formation of the Canon of the New Testament*, pub. by the American Sunday School Union 1892. In *The Inspiration and Authority of the Bible*, Presbyterian and Reformed Pub. Co., Philadelphia, 1948. Dated but a clear and careful defence of the canon.

Wenham, John W. *Christ and the Bible*, Tyndale Press, London, 1972. A useful book, though the reader would be better with F. F. Bruce.

Westcott, Brooke Foss. *The Canon of the New Testament During the First Four Centuries*, Macmillan & Co., Cambridge, 1855. Westcott was one of the greatest New Testament scholars of his day and his treatment of the canon is remarkably conservative. The date means that it cannot relate to more recent discoveries and theories, but the fundamental data has not changed since his time and he leaves practically no stone unturned.

Notes

Chapter 1

1. B. H. Cowper, *The Apocryphal Gospels and other Documents Relating to the History of Christ*, Williams and Norgate, London and Edinburgh, 1870, Preface.
2. As above, Introduction p.x.
3. Ellicott, *Cambridge Essays*, 1856, p.155.
4. B. F. Westcott, *The Canon of the New Testament During the First Four Centuries*, Macmillan & Co., Cambridge,1855, p.8.
5. A helpful summary will be found in Thiede, *The Jesus Papyrus*, pp.135–8.
6. Irving Wallace, *The Word*, Cassell & Co., London, 1972, p.89.
7. As above, p.464.
8. Baigent, Leigh and Lincoln, *The Holy Blood and the Holy Grail*, Gorgi Edition, 1983, pp.405, 333.
9. Dan Brown, *The Da Vinci Code*, Transworld Publishers (Bantam Press), London, 2003, p.231.
10. As above.
11. As above, p.235.
12. Richard Dawkins, *The God Delusion*, Transworld Publishers (Bantam Press), London, 2006, p.237.
13. As above, pp.92–93.
14. As above, pp.95–96. Here, incidentally, Dawkins confuses the Gospel of Thomas with the Infancy Gospel of Thomas.
15. *Jesus the Man: Decoding the Real Story of Jesus and Mary Magdalene; The Book That Jesus Wrote: John's Gospel; Jesus of*

the Apocalypse: The Life of Jesus After the Crucifixion to name just three.

16. John Allegro, *Sacred Mushroom and the Cross*, Hodder and Stoughton Ltd, London, 1970.
17. A more detailed assessment of the history of biblical criticism will be found in Brian Edwards, *Nothing But The Truth*, Evangelical Press, Darlington, 2006, pp.9–37.
18. John A. T. Robinson, *Redating the New Testament*, SCM Press, London, 1976.
19. As above, p.13.
20. As above, p.85.
21. As above, p.86.
22. As above, p.254.
23. As above, p.70.
24. As above, p.1.
25. As above, p.229.
26. As above, p.341.
27. As above, p.9.
28. As above, pp.341,345.
29. As above, p.342.
30. As above, p.343.
31. Thiede, *The Jesus Papyrus*, Wesidenfeld & Nicolson, London, 1996, p.135.
32. As above, pp.201–202.
33. J. B. Mayor, *The Epistle of St Jude and Second Epistle of St Peter*, 1907. Quoted in Donald Guthrie, *New Testament Introduction*, Tyndale Press, London, 1962, Vol. 3, p.162.
34. A. Q. Morton, 'Statistical Analysis and New Testament Problems' in *The Authorship and Integrity of the New Testament*, SPCR Theological Collection, 1965. Quoted in Robinson, *Redating the New Testament*, p.185.
35. See the *National Geographic* magazine time-line at http://www.nationalgeographic.com/lostgospel/timeline.html though their documentary on the National Geographic Channel claimed 'between 60 to 80 AD'.
36. The earliest tradition is that Luke died at the age of 84 in Greece where he wrote his Gospel. This is not impossible since he could have been around 60 when he travelled with Paul.
37. B. F. Westcott, *The Canon of the New Testament*, p.542.
38. Clement of Alexandria, *The Miscellanies,* Book VI, 15. He

comments: 'The ecclesiastical rule (canon) is the concord and harmony of the Law and the Prophets.'

39. Westcott, *The Canon of the New Testament*, p.548, referring to Origen's commentary on Matthew 28: 'no one should use for the proof of doctrine books not included among the canonized Scriptures'.

40. John Calvin, *Institutes of the Christian Religion*. Trans. Henry Beveridge, James Clark & Co. Ltd, London, 1962. Orig. 1536, Book I, Ch. 7:2,4.

41. Carl Henry, *God, Revelation and Authority*, Vol. IV, p.440.

42. John W. Wenham, *Christ and the Bible*, Tyndale Press, London, 1972, p.126. More than a century earlier, the respected New Testament scholar B. F. Westcott referred to 'the guidance of Providence' in his minute assessment of the development of the canon, *The Canon of the New Testament*, p.293.

43. Bruce Metzger, *The Canon of the New Testament*, Oxford University Press, Oxford, 1987, p.282.

44. As above, p.283.

Chapter 2

1. Contrary to Pfeiffer and Barclay, William Barclay, *The Making of the Bible*, Lutterworth Press, London, 1965, p.17.

2. The Apocrypha, 1 Maccabees 9:27, at the time of revolt against Syrian occupation in the mid second century BC by Judas Maccabeas: 'There was a great affliction in Israel, the like whereof was not since the time that a prophet was not seen among them.'

3. The Apocrypha, 1 Maccabees 14:41.

4. John W. Wenham, *Christ and the Bible*, Tyndale Press, London, 1972, p.145.

5. For a more detailed discussion of the Apocrypha see Brian Edwards, *Nothing But The Truth*, Evangelical Press, Darlington, 2006, pp.201–206.

6. The first explicit definition of the Catholic Canon is the Tridentine Canon of the Council of Trent, Session IV, 1546.

7. David Daniell, *The Bible in English*, Yale University Press, Newhaven & London, 2003, p.187.

8. For a full discussion on the Apocrypha in early editions of English Bibles see David Daniell, *The Bible in English*, Yale University Press, New Haven and London, 2003.

9. Josephus, *Against Apion*, translated by William Whiston, Ward, Lock & Co., London. No date given. Book 1, ch. 8.
10. Bruce points out that Josephus did allow the existence of prophets but not in the line of the biblical seers and thus not with additional Scripture. F. F. Bruce, *The Canon of Scripture*, InterVarsity Press, Illinois, 1988, p.33.
11. Eusebius, the first Christian historian writing in the mid fourth century, *De Pref. Evangel*, Book V, 3:6.
12. Wenham, *Christ and the Bible*, p.134.
13. Dennis C. Duling and Norman Perrin, *The New Testament, an Introduction: Proclamation and Parenesis, Myth and History*, Harcourt Brace Jovanovich, 1982, p.31. See also Charles Gore, Henry Leighton Goudge, Alfred Guillaume, *A New Commentary on Holy Scripture: Including the Apocrypha*, Book, Macmillan, 1936.
14. This is a widespread view. See for example R. Beckwith, *The Old Testament Canon of the New Testament Church*, SPCK, London, 1985, p.276. Also A. Bentzen, *Introduction to the Old Testament*, Copenhagen, 1948, Vol. 1, p.31; Bruce Metzger, *The Canon of the New Testament*, Oxford University Press, Oxford, 1987, p.110; John Wenham, *Christ and the Bible*, Tyndale Press, London, 1972, pp.138–9.
15. R. H. Charles, *The Apocrypha and Pseudepigrapha of the Old Testament*, Clarendon Press, Oxford, 1913, 2 vols., though some would add more.
16. Carl F. H. Henry, *God, Revelation and Authority*, Vol. IV, Paternoster, Carlisle, 1999 (orig. USA 1979), p.407.
17. A helpful response to this challenge will be found in *Hermeneutics, Authority and Canon*, ed. Carson and Woodbridge, IVP, London, 1986, pp.308–10.
18. Although translations of Enoch were known in Ethiopic and Greek, Aramaic fragments were discovered among the Dead Sea Scrolls (Q4). The Book of Enoch is generally thought to be dated around 200 BC. It claims to be prophecies of Enoch (Gen. 5). Jude clearly quotes from Enoch 1:9. Some scholars maintain that there are allusions to the book even in the teaching of Jesus, but this is doubtful.
19. For a more detailed discussion see F. F. Bruce, *The Canon of Scripture*, InterVarsity Press, Illinois, 1988, pp.43–54.
20. A collection of Jewish and Christian poems composed between

200 BC and AD 250. See J. J. Collins, *The Old Testament Pseudepigrapha*, ed. Charlesworth, pp.317–472.

21. This is a point made firmly by John W. Wenham in *Christ and the Bible*, pp.146-7.

Chapter 3

1. This point was made long ago by B. B. Warfield in *The Formation of the Canon of the New Testament*, pub. by the American Sunday School Union, 1892. Published in *The Inspiration and Authority of the Bible*, Presbyterian and Reformed Publishing Company, Philadelphia, 1948, p.411.
2. Polycarp, To the Philippians, Ch. 12.
3. As above, Ch. 7.
4. Clement's Second letter to the Corinthians, Ch. 2:8.
5. Ignatius, Epistle to the Philadelphians, Ch. 5.
6. Ignatius, Epistle to the Smyrnaeans, Ch. 7:4.
7. Ignatius, Epistle to the Magnesians, Ch. 12:8.
8. Tertullian, *De Praescriptione Haereticorum* (On the Prescription of Heretics), Ch. 36.
9. Warfield, *Canon*, p.415.
10. *The first Apology of Justin Martyr to the Emperor Titus*, Ch. 47.
11. Carl Henry, *God, Revelation and Authority*, Vol. IV, p.438.
12. Eusebius, *Church History*, Book III, Ch. 24:6.
13. Xenophon, *Symposium*, 3.6.
14. B. B. Warfield expressed this well in *The Formation of the Canon of the New Testament*, p.415: 'From the time of Irenaeus down, the church at large had the whole Canon as we now possess it. And though a section of the church may not have been satisfied of the apostolicity of a certain book or of certain books; and though afterwards doubts may have arisen in sections of the church as to the apostolicity of certain books (as e.g. of Revelation): yet in no case was it more than a respectable minority of the church which was slow in receiving, or which came afterwards to doubt, the credentials of any of the books that then as now constituted the Canon of the New Testament accepted by the church at large.'
15. E. J. Goodspeed, *The Interpreter's Bible*, ed. G. A. Buttrick, Abingdon Press, New York, 1962, Vol. 1, p.68.
16. Eusebius, *Church History*, Book III, Ch. 24:6.

17. Carl Henry, *God, Revelation and Authority,* Paternoster Publishing, Carlisle, 1999, Vol. IV, p.409.
18. A point made also by F. F. Bruce, *The Canon of Scripture,* InterVarsity Press, Illinois, 1988, pp.278–9.
19. See chapter 9.
20. William Barclay, and other more liberal scholars of the New Testament, claim that around AD 90, 'There was a veritable epidemic of letter writing and something must have given it its impetus.' They provide the somewhat unlikely explanation that Paul's letters had been forgotten and were rediscovered! William Barclay, *The Making of the Bible,* Lutterworth Press, London, 1965, p.68. A far more likely explanation is that the churches woke up to the reality that they were in for the long haul.
21. Irenaeus, *Against Heresies,* Book III, Ch. 3:2, certainly referred to Rome as a leading church, but he made it clear that he was using it merely as an example because it was so well known and 'it would be very tedious … to reckon up the successions of all the Churches'.
22. Bruce Metzger, *The Canon of the New Testament,* Oxford University Press, Oxford, 1987, p.240.

Chapter 4
1. The *Didache,* 2:2
2. The *Didache,* 7:1–7.
3. Metzger, *The Canon of the New Testament,* Oxford University Press, Oxford, 1987, p.188.
4. Kirsopp Lake, *The Apostolic Fathers,* published London, 1912, vol. I, pp.337–339.
5. The Epistle of Barnabas, Ch. 9.
6. The Epistle of Barnabas, Ch. 9.
7. Metzger, p.236 from *De Perpetua Virginitate,* III,10.
8. The Shepherd of Hermas, Vision 3, Ch. 6.
9. Metzger, *The Canon of the New Testament,* p.65.
10. The Muratorian Canon, 75–81 in Bruce Metzger, *The Canon of the New Testament,* Appendix IV, p.307.
11. Tertullian, *On Modesty,* Ch. 10.
12. Origen, *Commentary on Romans,* 10:31.
13. Irenaeus, *Against Heretics,* Book III, Ch. 3:3.
14. As above.

Notes

15. Clement's letter to the Corinthians, Ch. 1.
16. As above, Ch. 7.
17. As above, Ch. 15.
18. As above, Ch. 20.
19. As above, Ch. 21.
20. As above, Ch. 35.
21. As above, Ch. 37.
22. As above, Ch. 44.
23. As above, Ch. 57.
24. According to Eusebius in his *Ecclesiastical History*, Book iii, Ch. 16. He describes it as 'of considerable length and of remarkable merit'. Dionysius of Corinth, around AD 165, refers to the fact that the letter from Clement was still read for valuable 'admonition' — *Ecclesiastical History*, Book IV, Ch. 23:11.
25. Ignatius, The Epistle to the Romans, 14:2–5; 5:14–15.
26. As above, Ch. 3.
27. As above, Ch. 7.
28. Ignatius to the Philadelphians, Ch.6.
29. Ignatius to the Magnesians, 8:1.
30. The Martyrdom of Polycarp, 9:12.
31. The Epistle of Polycarp to the Philippians, 3:2–3.
32. His own story is largely told in his second *Apology*, Chs. 3 and 12.
33. Justin Martyr, first *Apology*, Chs. 6 and 42.
34. As above, Ch. 27.
35. Justin Martyr, second *Apology*, Ch. 3.
36. As above, Chs. 14–15.
37. Justin Martyr, first *Apology*, Ch. 59.
38. Stählin in Metzger, *The Canon of the New Testament*, p.131.
39. Clement of Alexandria, *The Exhortation*, Book I, Ch. 7.
40. Clement of Alexandria, *The Instructor*, Book I, Ch. 2.
41. As above, Book II, Ch. 1.
42. Clement of Alexandria, *The Miscellanies*, Ch. 10.
43. Aristides, *Apology*, Ch. 12.
44. The challenge of Athenagoras is: 'Three things are alleged against us: atheism, Thyestean feasts, Oedipodean intercourse. But if these charges are true, spare no class: proceed at once against our crimes; destroy us root and branch, with our wives and children, if any Christian is found to live like the brutes.' Athenagoras, *A Plea for the Christians*, Ch. 3.

45. Athenagoras, *A Plea for the Christians*, Ch. 32.
46. As above, Ch. 37.
47. Eusebius, *Church History*, Book V, Ch. 19:5–7. Translated by Paul L. Maier, *Eusebius: The Church History*, Kregel Publications, Grand Rapids, 1999, p.195.
48. Irenaeus, *Against Heresies*, Book I, Ch. 10:2.
49. As above, I, Preface 2.

Chapter 5

1. G. M. Hahneman, in *The Muratorian Fragment and the Development of the Canon*, OUP, Oxford, 1992, has suggested that it is a fourth-century document; however, this is not generally accepted.
2. The Muratorian Canon. Trans. Roberts-Donaldson Translation: *Ante-Nicene Fathers*, vol. 5, Section 1. See also a translation in F. F. Bruce, *The Canon of Scripture*, InterVarsity Press, Illinois, 1988, pp.159–161, and Metzger, *The Canon of the New Testament*, OUP Clarendon Press, Oxford, 1987, pp.305–307.
3. Through a copyist's error this could be a reference to the epistles of Peter. See Bruce, *The Canon of Scripture*, p.165, though 1 Peter was widely accepted.
4. As above, Section 3.
5. Epistle of Clement to the Corinthians, Ch. 1:1.
6. Epistle of Ignatius to the Romans, 4:8–10.
7. Epistle of Polycarp to the Philippians, 3:2.
8. As above, 6:5.
9. Metzger, *The Canon of the New Testament*, p.73, is probably right to suggest that at this stage 'we find the beginning of a movement, unconscious at first' towards accepting the primacy of the words of Jesus preserved in books.
10. The Epistle of Barnabas, Ch. 4:14.
11. The Epistle of Barnabas, Ch. 4:12.
12. Papias, *From the Exposition of the Oracles of the Lord*, Ch. 1. We are reliant on the fourth-century church historian, Eusebius, for much of our information about Papias. See Eusebius, *Ecclesiastical History*, Book III, Ch. 39:3–4, 'The Writing of Papias'.
13. Papias, *Fragments* III.
14. Papias, *From the Exposition of the Oracles of the Lord*, Ch. 6. As above, *Ecclesiastical History*, 16.

Notes

15. The Epistle of Ignatius to the Ephesians, Ch. 6.
16. Ignatius to the Romans, Ephesians, Traillians, Magnesians and Smyrneans.
17. Ignatius to the Magnesians, 12:8.
18. Westcott says that Polycarp 'contains far more references to the writings of the New Testament than any other work of the first age', Westcott, *The Canon of the New Testament*, p.44.
19. Westcott, *The Canon of the New Testament*, p.44.
20. The Epistle of Polycarp to the Philippians, Chs. 2 and 7.
21. As above, Ch. 4.
22. As above, Ch. 7.
23. Bruce Metzger, *The Canon of the New Testament*, p.62.
24. The Epistle of Polycarp, Ch. 3.
25. As above, Ch. 11.
26. As above, Ch. 12.
27. As above, Ch. 13.
28. Clement of Rome to the Corinthians, 46.
29. As above, 47.
30. As above, 56.
31. Metzger, *The Canon of the New Testament*, p.67.
32. The Second Epistle of Clement, 2:7–8. Though not from Clement, some date it as early as AD 98 – 100.
33. Justin's first *Apology*, Ch. 67.
34. *Justin to Trypho*, Ch. 106.
35. As above, Ch. 103.
36. As above, Ch. 49.
37. Justin's first *Apology*. See Chs 15 to 17 in particular.
38. Westcott, *The Canon of the New Testament*, p.141.
39. Bishop Rabbula of Edessa and Theodoret of Cyrrhus. The latter found 200 copies which he removed and replaced with the four Gospels.
40. Eusebius, *Ecclesiastical History*, Book IV, Ch. 23:12. Also Fragments of letter of Dionysius to the church at Rome.
41. Aristides, *Apology*, Ch. 2.
42. Aristides, Apology, Ch. 16.
43. Westcott, *The Canon of the New Testament*, p.250, agrees with this, but also adds that 'The form of Christian doctrine current throughout the church, as represented by men most widely differing in national and personal characteristics, in books of the most varied aim and composition, is measured exactly by

the Apostolic Canon.' In other words, the theology of all these early writers agrees with the New Testament.

44. Westcott concludes: 'Scarcely a fragment of the earliest Christian literature had been preserved which does not contain some passing allusion to the Apostolic writing; and yet in all there is no discrepancy. The influence of some common rule is the only natural explanation of this common consent.' *The Canon of the New Testament*, pp.365, 368.

Chapter 6

1. Bruce Metzger, *The Canon of the New Testament*, Oxford University Press, Oxford, 1987, p.157.
2. Irenaeus, *Against Heresies*. For example, in Book III, ch. 17:4, Irenaeus refers to 'Texts of Holy Scripture used by these heretics to support their opinions' which reveals Irenaeus' clear acceptance of the Gospels and the apostles as 'Holy Scripture'.
3. As above, Book III, Ch. 11:7–8.
4. As above, Book III, Ch. 1:1.
5. As above.
6. As above, Book III, Ch. 3:3.
7. F. F. Bruce, *The Canon of Scripture*, InterVarsity Press, Illinois, 1988, p.177.
8. Tertullian, *The Prescription Against Heretics*, Ch. 36.
9. Tertullian, *Against Marcion*, Book IV, Ch. 2.
10. Tertullian, *The Prescription Against Heresies*, Ch. 14.
11. Tertullian, *Modesty,* Ch. 20.
12. As above.
13. Tertullian, *Apologetic*, Ch. 20.
14. Tertullian, *The Prescription Against Heretics*, Ch. 4.
15. Tertullian, *Against Marcion*, Book V, Ch. 2.
16. Tertullian, *The Prescription Against Heretics*, Ch. 6.
17. Metzger, *The Canon of the New Testament*, citing the work of von Soden (Leipzig 1909).
18. Cyprian, *On the Lord's Prayer*, 1. Clearly the influence of Hebrews 1:1–2.
19. See Bruce Metzger, *The Canon of the New Testament*, p.150, though Metzger does not necessarily subscribe to this view. Hippolytus was the last of the great leaders in the West to use Greek as his language of writing.
20. As above, pp.131,133–4. Quoting the work of Otto Stählin.

Notes

21. Clement of Alexandria, *Stromata* (Miscellanies), Book 1, Ch. 1.
22. F. F. Bruce, *The Canon of Scripture*, p.180.
23. Clement of Alexandria, *Instructor*, Ch. 5.
24. Clement of Alexandria, *Stromata*, Book VI, Ch. 11.
25. Eusebius, *Ecclesiastical History*, VI,14.
26. Alexander Souter, *The Canon of the New Testament*, Duckworth & Co., London, 1913, p.174.
27. Origen, *De Principiis* (Concerning Principles), Preface 4. He used the title 'New Testament' six times in *De Principiis*.
28. Origen, *De Principiis*, Ch. 1:6.
29. Origen, *De Principiis*, Preface, 4, and Ch. 3:1.
30. So writes Eusebius in *Ecclesiastical History*, VI, Ch. 35:4.
31. Origen, *Homilies in Jos*, VII, 1.
32. An intriguing comment by Eusebius (*Ecclesistical History*, Book V, Ch. 10) refers to Pantaenus, a teacher of Clement in Alexandria, 'a man highly distinguished for his learning' who 'is said to have gone to India. It is reported that among persons there who knew of Christ, he found the Gospel according to Matthew, which had anticipated his own arrival. For Bartholomew, one of the apostles, had preached to them, and left with them the writing of Matthew in the Hebrew language, which they had preserved till that time.' It is impossible to verify this account.
33. Eusebius, *Ecclesiastical History*, Book III, 25 and following, for his full lists.
34. Metzger, *The Canon of the New Testament*, p.205.
35. Westcott, *The Canon of the New Testament*, pp.467–8.
36. From the *Festal Epistle* of Athanasius XXXIX. Translated in *Nicene and Post-Nicene Fathers*, Vol. IV, pp.551,552.
37. For the detail of some of these later writers see Metzger, *The Canon of the New Testament*, pp.212–7, and Bruce, *The Canon of Scripture*.
38. Jerome, *Letter to Hedeba*, 406–7.
39. Bruce, *The Canon of the Scriptures*, p.229.
40. Augustine's list can be found in *Of The Doctrine of Christ*, Book II, 12:8. It agrees exactly with our canon.
41. Augustine, *On Christian Learning*, 2:12.
42. Westcott in *The Canon of the New Testament*, p.292, comments on the translations into Syrian and Latin before the close of

the second century: 'Combined with the original Greek they represent the New Testament Scriptures as they were read throughout the whole of Christendom towards the close of second century.'

43. Metzger, *The Canon of the New Testament*, p.220. Parts of the churches in Syria to this day accept only twenty-two books. See F. F. Bruce, *The Canon of Scripture*, p.215.
44. Westcott, *The Canon of the New Testament*, p.540.
45. Metzger, p.107.
46. Eusebius, *Ecclesiastical History*, Book VIII, Ch. 2:4.

Chapter 7
1. F. F. Bruce, *The Canon of Scripture*, InterVarsity Press, Illinois, 1988, p.168.
2. Irenaeus, *Against Heresies,* Book I, Ch. 18:1.
3. As above, Ch. 21:5.
4. Tertullian, *Against Marcion*, Book V.
5. Tertullian, *On Baptism*, Ch.17.
6. The Muratorian Canon, Section 3. See chapter 5 for details of this canon.
7. For an analysis of Marcion's editing see F. F. Bruce, *The Canon of Scripture*, pp.134–144.
8. *The Martyrdom of Polycarp*, 22:18.
9. Justin, *The first Apology*, Ch. 58.
10. F. F. Bruce, *The Canon of Scripture*, p.148.
11. Bruce Metzger, *The Canon of the New Testament*, Oxford University Press, 1987, p.99.
12. Irenaeus, *Against Heresies,* Book 3, Ch. 11.7.
13. Tertullian, *The Prescription Against Heresies*, Ch. 14.
14. Irenaeus, *Against Heresies,* Book 3, Ch. 17:4.
15. As above, Ch. 38.
16. As above, Book 1, Ch. 14:3-7.
17. As above, Book 1, Ch. 24:3.
18. As above, Book 1, Ch. 24:4.
19. As above, Book 1, Ch. 25:1. 'They also hold that Jesus was the son of Joseph, and was just like other men, with the exception that he differed from them in this respect, that … he perfectly remembered those things which he had witnessed.'
20. As above.
21. As above, Book 1, Ch. 20:1.

Notes

22. As an example, the story of Simon substituting for Jesus on the cross is referred to in the Koran, ch. 4, 158.
23. Irenaeus, *Against Heresies*, Book 1, Ch. 31:1.
24. *The Gospel of Judas*, ed. Kasser, Meyer and Wurst, The National Geographic Society, 2006.
25. Irenaeus refers to her cult more than thirty times and mocks the stupidity of Gnostic beliefs concerning her.
26. B. H. Cowper, *The Apocryphal Gospels and other Documents Relating to the History of Christ*, Williams and Norgate, London and Edinburgh, 1870, pp.128–69. All of these apocryphal books can be read on line by searching under their title, but I have sometimes chosen to quote from a nineteenth-century volume to emphasize that there is nothing new in our knowledge of them.
27. Cowper, *The Apocryphal Gospels*, pp.29–83.
28. See Wesley Center Online. Hosted by the Northwest Nazarine University, Idaho, 1993-2005, the Gospel of Peter XV.
29. See Wesley Center Online, the Gospel of the Lord.
30. B. H. Cowper, *The Apocryphal Gospels and other Documents Relating to the History of Christ*, p.100.
31. Cowper, *The Apocryphal Gospels*, p.105.
32. This comes from Eusebius' *Ecclesiastical History*, Book V, ch. xvii.17, and is certainly an exaggeration!
33. Eusebius' *Ecclesiastical History*, Book V, ch.xvi. The actual words are: 'I have hesitated till the present time, not through lack of ability to refute the falsehood or bear testimony for the truth, but from fear and apprehension that I might seem to some to be making additions to the doctrines or precepts of the Gospel of the New Testament, which it is impossible for one who has chosen to live according to the Gospel, either to increase or to diminish.'
34. In *The Apocryphal Gospels*, Cowper refers to his own work and that of others and concludes that at the most there are 'some probable traces of the Apocryphal Gospels' (p.xx) in the writings of the church Fathers — but no more than this.
35. Cowper, *The Apocryphal Gospels*, p.53.
36. A useful survey of this subject in B. H. Cowper, *The Apocryphal Gospels*, Introduction, pp. xxviii-xlvii.
37. Cowper, *The Apocryphal Gospels*, p.xlv.
38. C. S. Lewis, *Christian Reflections*, Eerdmans, Grand Rapids,

1967, p.150.

39. Bruce Metzger, *The Canon of the New Testament*, p.166.
40. As above, p.173.
41. B. H. Cowper, *The Apocryphal Gospels*, p.xxv.
42. Bishop Ellicott, *Cambridge Essays,* 1856, p.157. Quoted in Cowper, *The Apocryphal Gospels*, p.xlvii.

Chapter 8

1. Bruce Metzger, *The Canon of the New Testament*, Oxford University Press, 1987, p.77.
2. Irenaeus, *Against Heresies,* Book I, ch. 18, 1.
3. Quotations from the Gnostic Society Library on line, the Gospel of Truth from *Gnosticism,* Harper & Brothers, New York, 1961. Translated by Robert M. Grant.
4. *Against Heresies,* Book III, chap.11:9.
5. John Wenham, quoting van Unnik in *Christ and the Bible*, Tyndale Press, London, 1972, p.154.
6. Quotations from the Gospel of Thomas from the Gnostic Society Library on line. James M. Robinson, ed. The Nag Hammadi Library. Revised edition. HarperCollins, San Francisco, 1990. Translated by Thomas O. Lambdin.
7. Bruce Metzger, *The Canon of the New Testament*, p.272. He continues that in this false gospel: 'The voice of the Good Shepherd is heard in only a muffled way, and that it is, in fact, often distorted beyond recognition by the presence of supplementary and even antagonistic voices.'
8. Quotations from the Gnostic Society Library on line. James M. Robinson ed. The Nag Hammadi Library. Revised edition, HarperCollins, San Francisco, 1990. Translated by Wesley W. Isenberg.
9. As above, The Gospel of Philip. Translated by Wesley W. Isenberg.
10. As above, The Gospel of Mary. Translated by George W. Macrae and R. Mc L.Wilson.
11. As above, The Gospel of the Egyptians. Translated by Alexander Bohlig and Frederik Wisse.
12. As above, the *Apocryphon* of James. Translated by Francis E. Williams.
13. Irenaeus, *Against Heresies*, Book I, Ch. 31:1.
14. F. F. Bruce, *The Canon of Scripture*, p.251.

Notes

Chapter 9

1. Sir Frederick Kenyon, *Handbook to the Textual Criticism of the New Testament*, 2nd ed., Eerdmans, Grand Rapids, 1953, p.35.
2. F. F. Bruce, *The Books and the Parchments*, Pickering & Inglis, London, 1950, p.170.
3. Bruce Metzger, *The Text of the New Testament*, OUP, Oxford, 1992, third ed., p.206.
4. See Bruce Metzger, *The Text of the New Testament*, pp.15–6. William Barclay, *The Making of the Bible*, Lutterworth Press, London, 1965, p.46.
5. These texts are in order of age: *Wissenburgensis 22*. Codex *Parisinus Graecus* Gr. 1419 and Parchment *Saragossa Nr. 253 in Greek*. They can be found from Roger Pearse at: http://www.tertullian.org/rpearse/manuscripts/josephus_all.htm.
6. It is known as The Papyrus Vindobonensis 29810.
7. Details of the extant MSS of Tacitus can be found at: http://www.tertullian.org/rpearse/tacitus/index.htm
8. T. Rice Holmes (ed.). C. Iuli Caesaris Commentarii. Rerum in Gallia Gestarum VII, A. Hirti Commentarius VIII. Oxford, 1914, pp.xii-xiv.
9. See Kurt Aland and Barbara Aland, *The Text of the New Testament*. Trans. E. F. Rhodes, Eerdmans, Grand Rapids, 1987, p.99. However, Bruce Metzger, *The Text of the New Testament*, p.38, opts for a date in the middle or late third century.
10. See Y-K. Kim, 'Paleographic Dating of P46 to the later First Century' in *Biblica*, 69 (1988), pp.248–57. Quoted in *The Jesus Papyrus*, pp.94,173. Bruce Metzger contradicts Kim in *The Text of the New Testament*, OUP, 1992, third ed., pp.264–5.
11. See Bruce Metzger, *The Text of the New Testament*, p.39, note 2.
12. Quote from H. Guppy, *Transmission of the Bible* (1935), p.4, in F. F. Bruce, *The Books and the Parchments*, Pickering & Inglis, London, 1950, p.172.
13. Thiede and D'Ancona, *The Jesus Papyrus*, Weidenfeld and Nicolson, London, 1996, pp.104–5.
14. Bruce Metzger, *The Text of the New Testament*, p.39.
15. *The Jesus Papyrus*, p.124, and see the work of Herbert Hunger, p.174, note 2. Also Metzger, *The Text of the New Testament*, p.40, note 1.

16. Eusebius, *The Life of Constantine*, IV, 36.
17. Alexander Souter, *The Text and Canon of the New Testament*, Duckworth & Co., London, 1913, p.36.

Chapter 10
1. Sir Frederick Kenyon, *The Story of the Bible*, John Murray, London, 1949, p.14.
2. Bruce Metzger, quoted in Estrada and White, *The First New Testament*, Thomas Nelson Inc., New York, 1978, p.79, but not referenced.
3. Thiede and D'Ancona, *The Jesus Papyrus*, Weidenfeld and Nicolson, London, 1996, p.55. Note that the defence by Thiede and D'Ancona of the general conclusions of O'Callaghan were after the intervention of more than two decades of debate on the subject; there can be little more information to come to light. Detractors have had their opportunity. Strangely, in a generally useful book *Archaeology and the New Testament* (Baker Book House, Michigan, 1991), John McRay spends only twelve lines on the fragments of Qumran 7 and casually dismisses them as 'too scanty for positive identification'; he makes no mention of the scholarly confirmation by Thiede or Estrada even though the latest edition of his book in 2001 postdates their work.
4. By the respected British scholar Colin H. Roberts, though it has to be said that Roberts dismissed O'Callaghan's identification of the text as 'an exercise not in scholarship but in fantasy'. See *The First New Testament*, p.27. Was this a churlish response by one scholar who failed to identify the text where another succeeded?
5. Estrada and White, *The First New Testament*, p.123. See especially their conclusions on pp.126-31.
6. See particularly *Los papiros Griegos de la Cueva 7 de Qumran* (Madrid 1974). But a detailed discussion of his results in English will be found in Estrada and White, *The First New Testament*. On the other hand, Bruce Metzger in *The Text of the New Testament*, OUP, 1992, third ed., pp.264–5, disputes O'Callaghan's identification as merely 'interesting coincidences', though Thiede, Estrada and others have answered all his objections.
7. *The Jesus Papyrus*, p.56.

Notes

8. For a more cautious, though positive treatment, see *The Jesus Papyrus*, pp.125-6.
9. John Wenham, *Redating Matthew, Mark and Luke*, Hodder & Stoughton, London, 1991, p.179.
10. D. F. Strauss, *The Life of Jesus*. Trans. from the German, Chapman, London, 1846, Vol. 1, p.88.
11. His story is told in detail, together with the account of the identification of these P64 fragments, in Thiede and D'Ancona, *The Jesus Papyrus*.
12. *Harvard Theological Review*, 1953, no. 46, pp.233-7.
13. I. Gallo, *Greek and Latin Papyrology*, London, 1986, p.14. Quoted by Thiede, *The Jesus Papyrus*, p.106.
14. Thiede and D'Ancona, *The Jesus Papyrus*, pp.111-2.
15. Thiede and D'Ancona, *The Jesus Papyrus*, p.112.
16. Thiede and D'Ancona, *The Jesus Papyrus*, p.135.
17. John A. T. Robinson, *Redating the New Testament*, SCM Press, London, 1976, p.342.
18. In the Gregory-Aland list of New Testament papyri.
19. Thiede and D'Ancona, *The Jesus Papyrus*, p.89.
20. As above, pp.89-91.

Chapter 11
1. See chapter 1 for these quotation sources.
2. William Barclay, *The Making of the Bible*, Lutterworth Press, London, 1965, p.78.
3. Bruce Metzger, *The Canon of the New Testament*, Oxford University Press, Oxford, 1987, p.283.
4. William Barclay, *The Making of the Bible*, p.78.
5. Irenaeus, *Against Heresies*, Book III, Ch. 4:1.
6. Athanasius, *Festal Epistle* XXXIX.
7. Luther certainly questioned the right of James, Jude, Hebrews and Revelation to be in the canon. This was the weakness of a great mind because he could not square some of the teaching in these books with Paul — a problem not shared by most subsequent expositors.
8. John Wenham, *Christ and the Bible*, Tyndale Press, London, 1972, p.149.
9. Martin Franzman, *The Word of the Lord Grows*, Concordia Publishing House, St Louis, 1981, p.294.

10. For example, James Barr, *The Bible in the Modern World*, Harper & Row, New York, 1973.
11. Bruce Metzger, *The Canon of the New Testament*, p.285.

Appendix 2
1. Gregory, *Hymn*, I, 1,12:31.
2. John Wenham, *Christ and the Bible*, Tyndale Press, London, 1972, p.124.

General index

General index

General index

Marcion, 53, 57, 85, 90, 104, 130, 132, 133-6, 145-6, 153-5, 219
Mark, 89, 110, 112
 Gospel of, 15, 89, 95, 101, 105, 189-93, 198, 204, 208
Martyrdom of Isaiah, 37
Mary, mother of Jesus, 131, 143, 147
Mary Magdalene, 17, 19, 135, 144, 155, 161-3
Matthew, 54, 98, 112
 Gospel of, 15, 63, 89, 92-3, 95-101, 105, 194-6, 198
Matthew's Bible, 33
Mayor, J. B., 23
Melito, Bishop of Sardis, 40, 179
Metzger, Bruce, 28, 64, 66, 97, 108, 121, 127, 134, 151, 159, 175, 180, 201, 211
miniscule, 7, 9, 172-3
Montanists, 52, 107, 111, 130, 148-9
Montanus, 130, 148-9, 220
Montevecchi, Orsolina, 192
Moore, George, 14
Mormons, 59, 210
Morton, A.Q., 23
Moses, 30, 35-6, 79
Muratori, Ludovico, 89
Muratorian Canon, 47, 50, 53, 55, 59, 66-7, 89-90, 91-2, 105, 107, 111, 114, 132, 149, 202, 204-5, 207, 209, 213, 216, 221

Nag Hammadi Library, 12-13, 50-1, 55, 85, 136, 142, 154-5, 158-9, 161-3, 166-8
National Geographic, 24, 137-8
New Testament, 11, 13-15, 17, 18-19-21, 24-6, 32, 48, 55-6, 64, 96, 101-4, 109, 113, 117, 171,
177-9, 182, 183, 185
 acceptance of, 53, 57-60, 89-92, 98, 107, 129, 201-13
 accuracy of, 25
 authority of, 28-9, 38, 50-1, 107, 157, 168, 200-5, 212
 canon, 14, 15, 18, 21, 25-8, 44-7, 50-52, 56-60, 62, 87, 89, 105, 110, 112-13, 116-17, 119, 122, 130, 134, 151-2, 171, 193, 209
 completion of, 18, 20, 21, 22, 29, 48, 50, 181, 182, 183, 213
 criticism of, 18-20, 52, 210
 dating of, 18-23, 176, 184, 187-98
 development of, 92, 149, 169-86, 187-98, 200, 203-13
 divine origin, 26-9, 110, 117, 210-2
 formation of, 27, 46, 58, 92, 178, 204
 quoted by church leaders, 107-29, 209-12
 writers, 20, 26, 39-40, 110
nominem sacrum, 8, 180, 195

O'Callaghan, Jose, 190-4
Old Testament, 30, 39, 44, 48-9, 53, 66, 69, 78, 87, 92-3, 100, 102, 105, 109-10, 114-5, 117, 133, 179, 182, 183
 acceptance of, 36, 39, 40, 42, 48, 53, 57
 authority of, 38, 91, 102
 canon, 26, 30, 31, 38, 40-42, 51, 122, 212
 completion of, 35, 37
Origen, 26, 40, 68, 93, 107, 116-9, 130, 204, 207-9, 218, 221

Also from the author

Nothing but
the Truth

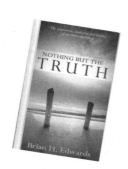

'The battle for the Bible continues. Liberal scholarship and sceptics continue to cast doubt upon the authenticity of all Scripture and its inerrancy. Here is a book rich enough in content to stir the minds and hearts of all who love the Bible and at the same time clear enough for all to understand the arguments so powerfully presented for the full and final authority of Scripture.'

Martin Holdt
Pastor of Constantia Park Baptist Church, Pretoria, South Africa

'Author Brian Edwards shows that it is perfectly reasonable ... and logical to believe in the Bible. It comes with my highest recommendation.'

Ken Ham
President and CEO, Answers in Genesis — USA

'If I could pass a law compelling every Christian to buy a copy I would do so immediately!'

John Blanchard
Author and international speaker

'The sheer scope of Edwards' writing, in this one book, is breathtaking and he does it in a manner suitable for the "common person in the pew".'

The English Churchman

Available from Evangelical Press, ISBN-13 978-0-85234-614-3.

A wide range of Christian books is available from Evangelical Press. If you would like a free catalogue please write to us or contact us by e-mail. Alternatively, you can view the whole catalogue online at our website:

www.evangelicalpress.org.

Evangelical Press
Faverdale North, Darlington, DL3 0PH, England

e-mail: sales@evangelicalpress.org

Evangelical Press USA
P. O. Box 825, Webster, New York 14580, USA

e-mail: usa.sales@evangelicalpress.org